Behind the screen of Naaz Cinema, Bombay.

ADVANCE BOOKING
10:00 A.M. TO 7:00 P.M.

UPPER STALL

SHOWS	FRI.	SAT.	SUN.	MON.	TUE.	WED.	THU.
3							
6:00							
9:30							

ADVANCE BOOKING FOR DAILY AT 11:30 AM Rs.

BEHIND THE SCENES
OF HINDI CINEMA

A visual journey through the heart of Bollywood

BY JOHAN MANSCHOT AND MARIJKE DE VOS

ACKNOWLEDGEMENTS

The authors would like to thank:
Nasreen Munni Kabir, for correcting the film index.
Ben Meulenbeld, South Asia Curator at the Amsterdam Tropenmuseum, for correcting the information on gods and goddesses.
Dick van der Meijden, for kindly lending us his huge LP collection.
Cilly Wolf, at Cilly Business, for some of the Tamil poster collage designs.
Sudha Rajagopalan, for the collection of Soviet posters.
Dick Plukker and Prem Radhakishun, for translating Hindi film titles.
Angelique's hands, for posing in the book.
The Perzische Supermarkt in Amsterdam, for providing us with Iranian video covers of Hindi films.
Mani Ratnam, for tolerating the taking of photographs on his crowded set.
Mr. Shaukat M. Khan, President of Mehboob Film Studios, for the beautiful posters and Mother India booklet, and for allowing us to take pictures of the Mehboob office and archive.
Mr. S. Rehman, for allowing us to take pictures in his studio.
Rakesh Sharma, manager of Naaz Cinema.
Fakhri Traders, Z. Hasan Khan (Zain Cine Poster Supplier), Abid Hussain Vora (Farida Traders), and Frank (CasaBlanca).
Annemarie Manschot, for searching for posters and beating down prices.
KIT Tropentheater for its early and steady support of Indian cinema.
Frank Vermeer at KIT Publishers, for believing in this book.
And last but not least, our families, for their patience and putting up with many late night working sessions.

CITY NAMES

Wherever possible, in this book we have employed the city names in general local use: 'Chennai' rather than 'Madras', 'Kolkata' rather than 'Calcutta' and 'Bombay' rather than 'Mumbai'.

PREVIOUS PAGES:
Mera Vachan Geeta Ki Qasam
Hotel
Mughal-e-Azam
Lagaan and Haqeeqat

CONTENTS

10 FOREWORD AMITABH BACHCHAN

14 PUBLICITY P.K. NAIR
Traditional and New Modes: Songbooks, Songs, Posters and the Internet.

36 CENSORSHIP P.K. NAIR
The Censor Certificate, First Image in Every Hindi Film. Colonial and Modern Issues.

40 DEVOTION DEEPA GAHLOT
Worship of God and Family, the Importance of a Blessing at the Start of a Film Production.

46 PRODUCTION BANNERS DEEPA GAHLOT
Production Companies and their Logos.

52 CREDITS DEEPA GAHLOT
Main Characters in Hindi Films: Hero, Heroine, Villain, Vamp, Mother, Director, Playback Singer, Composer, Lyricist and Choreographer.

64 ENTERTAINMENT & ESCAPISM GAYATRI CHATTERJEE
Is that all there is? Old and New Utopias and the Urge to Escape.

72 MYTHOLOGY & FOLKLORE MARIJKE DE VOS | FAREEDA
A Who's Who of the Gods. The Omnipresence of Gods in Indian Cinema. The Divine Couples Ram–Sita and Radha–Krishna as Role Models.

84 MARRIAGE SCENES GAYATRI CHATTERJEE
Marriages, Marriage Signs, Love Triangles and Divine Love.

92 THE ENEMY FAREEDA
The Changing Image of the Enemy from Colonial until Modern Times.

100 SONGS BRAHMANAND SINGH
A Short History of Song with Lyrics of Some Classic Hindi Film Songs.

118 TAMIL CINEMA SOUDHAMINI
The Significant Other: Inspiration and Confrontation.

130 DISTRIBUTION HADI TEHRANI | SUDHA RAJAGOPALAN | NASREEN MUNNI KABIR
Hindi Films are Shown All Over India and were Exported to Various Parts of the World from the 1950s Onwards.
For Instance to Iran and the Soviet Union. The West Followed Only Recently and Baptised the Hindi Film Industry 'Bollywood'.

148 REVIEW MARIJKE DE VOS
Critics, Audiences, the Box Office and Awards.

SONG TRANSLATIONS | FILM INDEX | SOURCES | PHOTOGRAPHS | ABOUT THE AUTHORS | COLOPHON

FOREWORD

BY: **AMITABH BACHCHAN**

Amitabh Bachchan in *Black* (2005)

For every story that our cinema unfolds on the big screen, there are other stories behind it... stories of how ideas were conceived, of how they were executed, of how the characters were transformed by unique casting, and of how new locations were altered by natural disasters. Costumes were sometimes invented to overcome the pressures of deadlines. And some dialogues that seemed unconvincing while performing them became immortal after the release of the film.

Innumerable precious moments guarded and treasured in the creative reservoirs of time...

The world of the cinemagoer is far removed from the world of the dream merchants, and yet the two are strangely interwoven. From a distance, the viewer is intimately involved in the magic and the madness that characterise show business.
Film buffs are like passionate lovers on the lookout for a new conquest. Their every visit to the cinema is the beginning of a new courtship. They never miss the signals. Their journey begins when they spot the first hoarding.
The image continues to haunt them in the weeks that follow – until they go through the 'experience' of watching the new release inside a movie theatre.
They weave their own version of the story in their solitary moments, and even though the film never lives up to their expectations, the obsessive voyage into fantasyland never ceases. They have been addicted to the seduction for years.
In the olden days, movie moguls sent messengers with drums to ignite the film fan's imagination before making official announcements. Later, stage performers travelling on ornately decorated bullock carts distributed pamphlets. And today, with the advent of new technologies, new modes of presentation are being explored.

Behind the Scenes of Hindi Cinema is an insightful journey into the complex worlds of fantasy and reality inhabited by creative artistes. India is a unique country that exists in multiple centuries simultaneously. This book unravels the various mysteries and contradictions embedded in our centuries-old tradition.

It explores the changing identity of the country from pre-independence to globalisation, the socio-political situation of the period, and the intellectual and cultural influences on the performing arts.

Using defined sections and relevant case studies, the authors analyse the emotional ingredients that form the essence of India and Indian cinema. Why is it that a country mature enough to choose its leader by plebiscite, needs censors to choose its entertainment? Why do young film-makers in the new millennium continue to name their studios and banners after their deities?

Indians express themselves through folklore and poetry. Our heritage provides us with songs associated with all festivals and seasons. This is reflected in our films, where we have songs for every situation: love, separation, triumph or war. Occasionally, an extremely popular song has become an allegory for a generation of film audiences. KL Saigal's '*Babul Mora*' became the celebrated farewell song of the 1930s, while '*Awaara Hoon*' by Mukesh became the voice of migrants in the 1950s.

After independence, the nation followed a progressive agenda, and there was an urge to modernise. Many films released at that time strived to create a paradise for their protagonists and, indirectly, for the audience. Cinemagoers longed to escape into the dream world. For the three hours spent in the cinema, the audience was suffused with a sense of freedom and reassurance.

In contrast to Hollywood, Hindi cinema worked within set parameters. Inspired by epic and folk theatre, the stories and their characters fell within broad stereotypes. The hero was an incarnation of valour and virtue, and the heroine was always submissive and supportive. She responded positively to the hero's overtures and ideology. The villain represented evil, the mother symbolised conscience, while the father was the undisputed patriarch – right or wrong.

Marriage was the ultimate goal of most romantic relationships explored in films. The process of falling in love and the obstacles preventing marriage were indicators of prevailing social stigmas and customs.

Seldom did films feature erotica that was unacceptable to social norms. Morality was sacrosanct. In stories about lovers who did not ultimately become man and wife, the protagonists were compared to the romantic pair, Radha and Krishna. When a story dealt with an ideal marital couple, their relationship was likened to the union of Ram and Sita, who were devoted to tradition.

A century has gone by, and even though Indian cinema has evolved almost beyond recognition, a good deal remains unchanged, much like our country. Perhaps these intricacies attract outsiders to our films. Some describe our films as celebrations of song and dance, some as stories of love and pathos, and some as exotic and aesthetic.

Having been a part of Indian cinema for 35 years, I wonder what could be so captivating about our movies that they should attract such diverse audiences and bridge cultural and linguistic divides. There must be something divine and unique in our portrayals that they appreciate and we overlook. One feels overwhelmed and humbled by this universal recognition.

Over the years, Africa, Russia and the Middle East have endorsed Indian films as lively alternatives to Hollywood films. Iranian audiences reveal that they love Hindi films because they make them forget their sorrows.

No matter where one travels in the world, one always meets people who idolise Hindi films and are hooked on our popular songs.

There is a definite shift in attitude towards Indian popular cinema and I am proud to be part of it.

Rakesh Bachchan

Daag and Geet

LP cover and booklet from a deluxe package from **Naseeb** (1981)

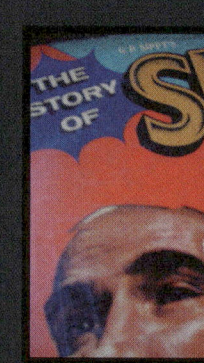

ABOVE FROM LEFT TO RIGHT: LP cover and booklet from **Amar Akbar Anthony** (1977) and **Shaan** LP and dialogue record (1980)

Mangalsutra (1981)

Jis Desh Men Ganga Behti Hai (1960)

PUBLICITY
BY P.K. NAIR

'These booklets turned out to be the authentic source material for verifying the cast, credits and plot outline of films.'

In the old days, maharajas and kings used drums or church bells to attract their *praja* (public) to make important announcements. Pamphlets advertising travelling circuses, magic shows and stage performances were distributed by pretty dancing girls, while they performed on ornately decorated bullock carts moving around the *basti* (village). Cinema reached out to an entertainment-hungry audience through various means: indigenous and sophisticated, traditional and modern, depending on the clientele.

Print media comes in handy

The Lumière brothers announced the first public demonstration of their new invention 'The Marvel of the Century', at Bombay's old Watsons Hotel on 7 July 1896, in a one-column insert in the *Times of India*, an English-language daily. Ever since, the print media, especially the daily press, has been the most accessible space available to film-makers for publicising their products and reaching an audience by way of advertisements or editorial. The one-column newspaper advertisements, which started with such catchy phrases as 'He came, he saw and she conquered' increased in size to include some imagery, usually of daredevil action and the attractive faces of the heroines, which provided viewers with an insight into what was in store.

The live performances that often preceded evening film programmes can be traced back to the Indian oral tradition of storytelling, and consisted of the *sutradaar* (performer) informing the audience of the contents of the

Song booklets and publicity folders

Song booklets, with elegantly illustrated covers containing stills from the film printed on special art paper, formed one of my most precious collections as a schoolboy in the early 1940s. They contained complete song lyrics, the cast list, technical credits and a brief synopsis in English and Hindi – and sometimes in Gujarati or Urdu. These booklets turned out to be the authentic source material for verifying the cast, credits and plot outline of films, and proved to be quite useful reference material for film researchers. Nowadays, publicity folders and brochures are produced containing synopses and directors' comments in English and other foreign languages. This has become necessary for the promotion of films in the export market and the festival circuit, in keeping with international practice. Some foreign distributors of Indian films brought out their own posters specially designed to suit local tastes. In a way, the song booklets and publicity folders fulfilled the role of the press books distributed to Indian exhibitors by the

'The worldwide popularity of Indian film songs has given a big boost to the music indus[try] monies invested in the film.'

Songs a great selling point

In the early days of cinema, records and cassettes of songs were put on the market at least six months before the release of the films in which they featured, and were broadcast extensively on the radio as advance publicity for them. As part of the government policy of giving preference to classical music, the Information and Broadcasting Minister, Keskar, banned the broadcast of film songs on All India Radio (AIR) for a brief period in the early 1950s. Radio Ceylon seized the opportunity and made Indian film songs popular, earning good revenue through commercials in the process. Later, AIR went all-out to the other extreme by introducing the exclusive twenty-four hour channel, *Vividh Bharathi*, primarily for broadcasting film songs. *Binaca Geet Mala*, the programme presented by Amin Sayani, became extremely popular and boosted the sales of discs and tapes, which in turn publicised the films. Doordarshan, the government's television network, carried the format forward, and the programmes *Chitrahaar* and *Chitrageet* attracted enormous numbers of viewers. Even now, programmes featuring film songs and film-based items are the most broadly popular ones on Indian channels.

The broadcast of songs on radio and television has become vital to the marketing of any Indian film.

The worldwide popularity of Indian film songs has given a big boost to the music industry. The revenues from sales of film music on CD and cassette is equal to a sizeable portion of the monies invested in the film. In the early days, only one or two dominant corporations such as HMV and Columbia were involved in the film songs business. Now their number is legion – resulting in cut-throat competition, piracy and blatant copyright violations. The audio industry has now started dictating terms to film-makers who can ill-afford to ignore them. The modern film song, then, must cater more to the music business' needs and demands than to the film itself. The number of remixes and music videos circulating has amply demonstrated that film songs can have an independent existence outside the framework of film. Only time will tell whether this phenomenon is good for cinema or not.

Hero (1983), **Insaan** (1982), **The Gold Medal** (1975), **Bobby** (1973), **Kranti** (1980), **Satyam Shivam Sundaram** (1978)

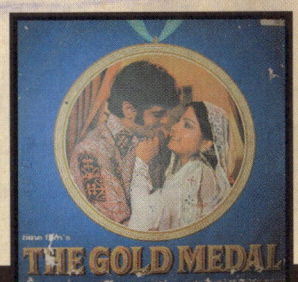
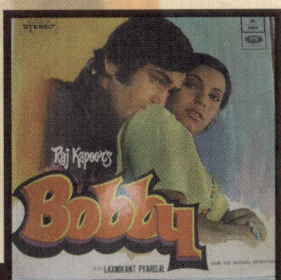

he revenues from sales of film music on CD and cassette is equal to a sizeable portion of the

'...start this magazine have been amply fulfilled over the years.'

Taken from editorial *'Seven Significant Years'*, (*Filmfare* magazine, 27 March 1959)

Covers and spreads from the early days (1953–54) *Filmfare* is still the most popular glossy film magazine.

'... the ceremony seems to have lost its sheen as people in the trade know for certain that out of every ten films launched with such fanfare and publicity, not more than five survive beyond the muhurat shot.'

Traditional ways and modes

Until recently, the launch ceremony for a new film was a big event popularly known as *muhurat* (auspicious moment). The muhurat ritual consists of breaking a coconut, lighting the sacred lamps, making an offering (*pooja*) to the Lord, garlanding the camera and microphone, and the clapperboard being prominently visible during the first shot. Finally, sweets are distributed to all those present and everyone is photographed for press publicity. Such muhurats were elaborately reported in the trade papers in the past. But now their sheen seems to have faded. Because, as people in the trade know for certain, of every ten films launched with such fanfare and publicity, not more than five survive beyond the muhurat shot. Such is the rate of infant mortality in the Indian film trade. So full-page advertisements or flamboyant muhurats do not guarantee that films will be completed and screened; it would be a miracle if they did. The situation is getting slightly better of late, with corporate bodies and industrial houses entering the scene and exercising a degree of economic discipline. Traditional muhurats have been replaced by functions celebrating the audio cassette release. These are usually held in five-star hotels in the presence of a celebrity such as Amitabh Bachchan, and are widely covered in both print and electronic media.

ABOVE: Amitabh Bachchan and his son Abhishel at the muhurat ceremony of *Ranveer*. Amar Singh gave the clap.
BELOW: Aamir Khan, Amitabh Bachchan and Rajkumar Santoshi.

Wall Posters

Street walls and print media continue to be the chief domains for film publicity. Colourful wall posters have long been one of the stock materials used by film-makers and distributors. Cinema posters of all sizes and designs splashed on street walls are a familiar sight as one walks along the main roads, lanes and alleys of any Indian city or small town. Even when local municipalities offer fixed display boards on lampposts and other selected spots, poster boys invariably prefer to go for the street walls they are familiar with – except in cases where the owner puts a 'stick no bills' sign on a freshly whitewashed wall. Traditionally, film posters come in three basic sizes, usually referred to as single-sheet (AO), double-sheet and six-sheet. The Motion Picture Export Association (MPEA), which imported American films into India, used to display twelve-sheet posters in front of the theatres they hired. For the average Indian film-maker or distributor even a six-sheeter is unaffordable, and they usually make do with single- and double-sheeters.

Even a cursory look at the design of Indian film posters will reveal that they adhere to a certain stereotyped graphic style in which the stars' faces dominate the theme and content. This might be attributable to the Indian narrative and visual tradition, in which content flows from the placement of faces, looks,

gestures and expressions at a frozen moment. The accent is always on stars' faces sporting stereotyped expressions that the viewer can easily identify with. The names of the director and musical director also feature prominently on the posters. The stars' faces are so familiar that their names hardly find mention on the posters, which are normally viewed from a distance.

LEFT: Yash Chopra's **Deewaar** (1975), six-sheet poster. Poster design by Bakshi.
MIDDLE: Guru Dutt's **Baharen Phir Bhi Aayengi** (1966), single-sheet poster. Poster design by Manohar.
RIGHT: **The Gold Medal** (1975), single-sheet poster. Directed by Ravi Nagaich. Poster design by unknown artist.

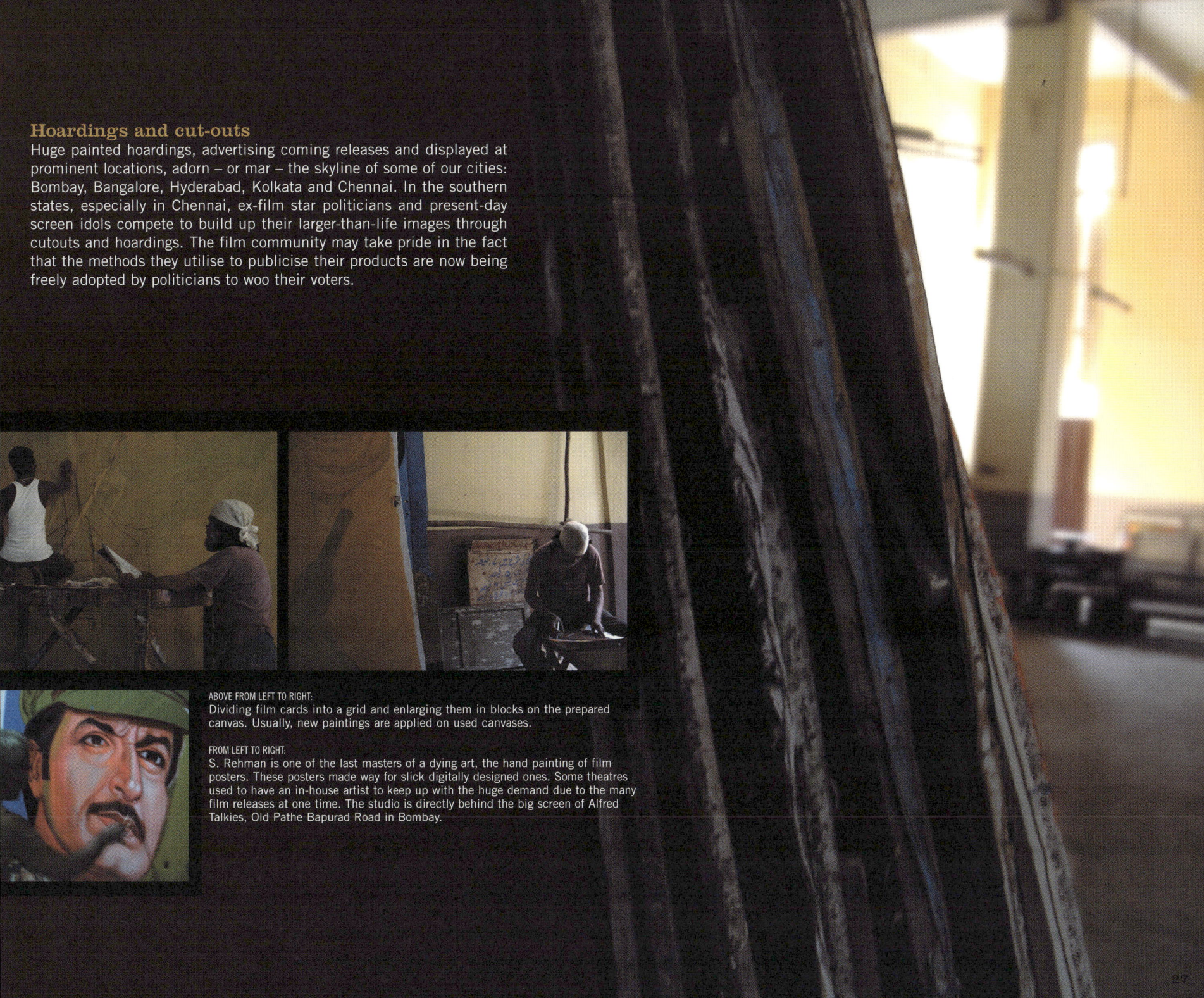

Hoardings and cut-outs

Huge painted hoardings, advertising coming releases and displayed at prominent locations, adorn – or mar – the skyline of some of our cities: Bombay, Bangalore, Hyderabad, Kolkata and Chennai. In the southern states, especially in Chennai, ex-film star politicians and present-day screen idols compete to build up their larger-than-life images through cutouts and hoardings. The film community may take pride in the fact that the methods they utilise to publicise their products are now being freely adopted by politicians to woo their voters.

ABOVE FROM LEFT TO RIGHT:
Dividing film cards into a grid and enlarging them in blocks on the prepared canvas. Usually, new paintings are applied on used canvases.

FROM LEFT TO RIGHT:
S. Rehman is one of the last masters of a dying art, the hand painting of film posters. These posters made way for slick digitally designed ones. Some theatres used to have an in-house artist to keep up with the huge demand due to the many film releases at one time. The studio is directly behind the big screen of Alfred Talkies, Old Pathe Bapurad Road in Bombay.

Large canvases waiting to be prepared and painted again.
E: The Alfred cinema with Rehman's on display in the streets of Bombay.

'The strong emphasis [in posters] on the human form, especially the face, is bound up with the evolution of Indian religious icons have taken on human form – male or female, and in some cases a combination of the main points of reference for practising devotees to establish contact with their spiritual aspirations. This ma film stars' faces in all sorts of moods, looks, poses and expressions in the Indian film poster.'

TEXT P.K. Nair from The International Poster Magazine (Issue 8, December 1993)

Commissioned work by *Balkrishna Art*, Bombay.
ABOVE: Detail from hand-painted poster for **Devdas**.

ABOVE AND RIGHT:
The love of film fans for their heroes has been compared to love for gods.
They express their devotion by garlanding them.

Non-traditional and new methods of publicity

With the advent of new technologies and the unprecedented expansion of television, new modes of transmission and presentation are being explored to reach out to the largest possible audience within the shortest time span. A classic television promotional advertisement I came across of late is for a Malayalam-language production in which superstar Mamootty, speaking to the camera, says 'This is the best Malayalam film I have seen to date. I am not in it. But I urge you to see it.' This low budget film turned out to be a runaway hit. All credit for the success of the film need not necessarily rest with this kind of promotion or any other, but it is important that the style of promotion matches the theme and integrity of the film. This kind of selective promotion is lacking in the Indian film industry. If the film is a break from the usual unexceptional fare, it needs a different kind of promotion. Television promotion is largely confined to the use of song and dance clips. This has become stale and monotonous, since one cannot distinguish one film from another – they all look alike, and so the intent of promotion is lost. Novel and alternative modes call for alternative films, as they are intrinsically interlinked. Let us hope the future provides exciting challenges for filmmakers and publicists.

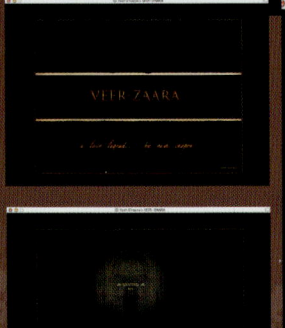
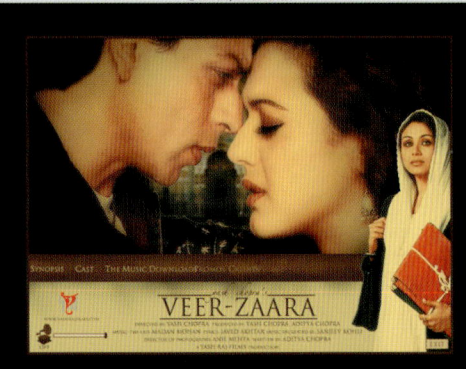
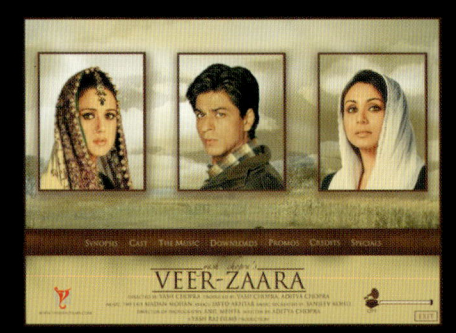

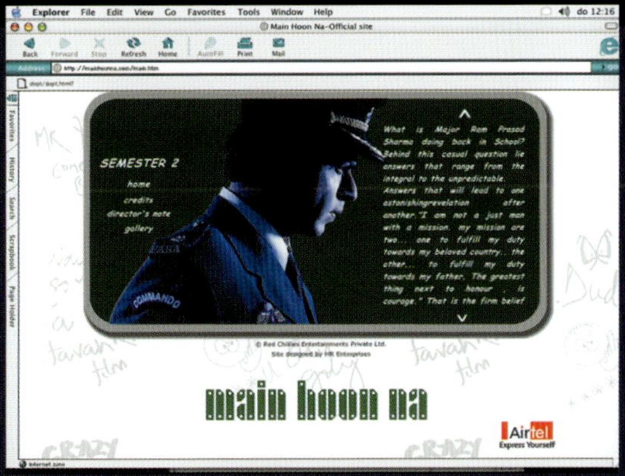

LEFT AND ABOVE:
Film trailers for **Veer-Zaara** and **Main Hoon Na** on the Internet.

CENSORSHIP
QUESTIONING FILM CENSORSHIP IN INDIA
BY: P.K. NAIR

The Beginning
Dadasaheb Phalke, the commonly accepted father of Indian cinema, was brought up in the ancient Vedic[1] tradition of spiritual pursuits. He was inspired by the wonder of film and its enormous potential to convey stories from the *Puranas* (epics) and spread the three basic tenets of Hinduism: truth, non-violence and religious tolerance. By launching *Swadeshi* film in 1913,[2] he instilled a sense of national pride in those with an involvement or interest in cinema – not only the film-makers but also the viewers. Indian cinema continues to maintain its national identity and is the most prolific of all national cinemas.

A throw of dice (1930)

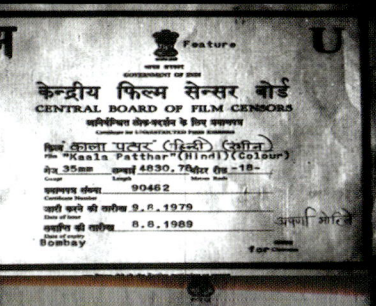
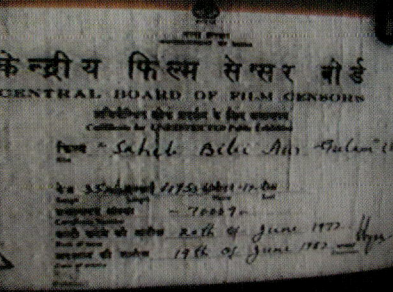
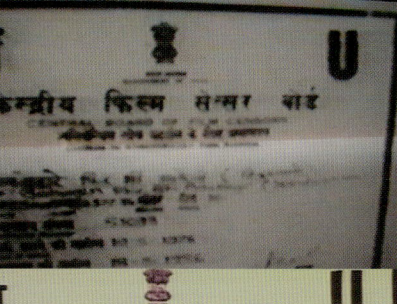
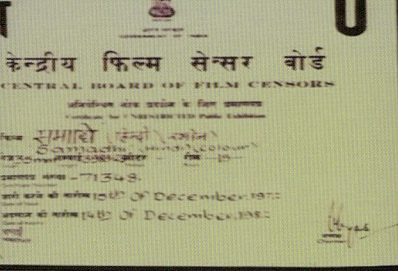
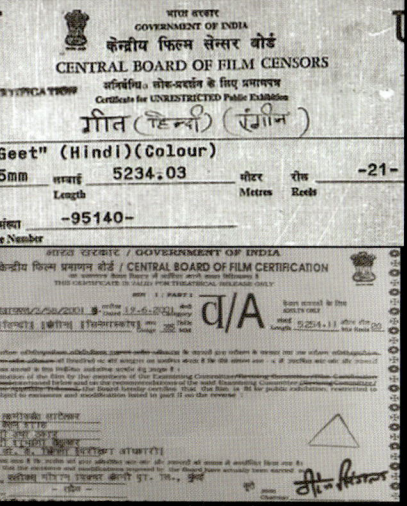

All proceeded smoothly in the early years of cinema until, towards the end of the First World War in 1918, a 'wise' guy in the British colonial regime thought it should have some influence on what was being screened in the nation's cinemas in the name of entertainment. Film content and context became controversial issues. In 1918, the Indian Cinematograph Act was passed. It introduced mandatory licensing of cinema houses to ensure audiences' safety and to prevent the showing of objectionable films.

The national government, which was established in 1947 – the year of independence from British rule – preserved this Act in order to justify its intervention in the film industry. In pre-independence India, censorship was the task of the local police chief, who was thus both political and cultural guardian of society in addition to his normal law-enforcement duties. During this period, five autonomous censor boards operated from as many cities: Bombay, Calcutta, Madras, Lahore and Rangoon. After independence, the national government merged them into a single monolithic entity, the Central Board of Film Censors (CBFC). The word 'Censors' has since been replaced by the less loaded 'Certification' – allowing the abbreviation to remain the same.

Colonial concerns

Increasing numbers of imported films from the West, especially America, started hitting Indian screens and influencing the national psyche. The colonial masters became concerned by the free flow of moving images of all shades and hues, from the puerile to the profane, the insipid to the mildly pornographic. The State had to intervene, and in 1920 a board of film censors drew up a set of general principles as guide-lines for the inspectors of films. These have remained part of the Indian cinema audience's experience ever since. Interestingly, pre- and post-independence censorship shared some characteristics, but there were some marked differences in perception too. For example, both systems vehemently objected to violence, and this was their main target. However, the British did not distinguish between violence in the context of valour and chivalry as depicted in an Indian *mythological*[3] by a character such as *Bhim* or *Arjun*,[4] and the sadistic violence in an American Western or crime thriller. They treated the two on equal terms, which might have embarrassed Indian viewers.

It is also strange that the British were unconcerned by onscreen displays of affection in the form of petting, hugging, caressing and, above all, kissing – in fact in the context of lovemaking it was not objected to at all. The taboo regarding kissing in Indian film only developed later. Kissing scenes were commonplace in the twenties and thirties; who can forget Sita Devi's passionate scenes in *Throw of Dice* (1929) or Devika Rani's in *Karma* (Duty, 1933), for example? Moreover, scenes depicting the baring of the female body were not rare.

Kissing disappeared from the Indian screen not because of censorship, but a collective, and self-imposed, decision by the patriotic film community, which did not wish to imitate Western culture or submit to its onslaught. This came at the peak of the freedom movement, and its public acceptance resulted from nationalist considerations and patriotic sentiments rather than anything else.

British priorities were different. They were more concerned with the proper depiction of the white man, especially the English, in Indian films. However, local film-makers resorted to subversive tactics, and caricatured the Westernised *England-returned*[5] character in *social*[6] films of the thirties and forties. In these tales, he is invariably portrayed as a stereotypical villain who uses foul means to usurp the native hero's girl, ultimately making a fool of himself. The England-returned stereotype thus represented the wily, the comic, the foolish and the rotten. The censors did not see through these jibes at Indians who took on traits of British culture. Nor did they reject the famous song '*Door Hatto, Door Hatto Duniyawalo Hindustan Hamara Hai*' (Keep away, keep away you foreigners, Hindustan belongs to us) from the Bombay Talkies' box office hit *Kismet* (Destiny,1943), which also contained the line 'We will never bow our head before anyone, whether Japanese or German.' Audiences of the time knew that the warning was directed at the British as well, although it was not spelt out in such clear terms as the reference to the Germans and Japanese. The film came at a time when India was in the thick of the freedom movement and the air was filled with 'Quit India'[7] slogans. As it was ostensibly a war-effort song the censors could do nothing about it, and the audiences made the song and the film the biggest box office grosser of its time. The colonial regime also disliked the fictionalised images of the national leaders Tilak, Gandhi, Nehru, Subhas Bose and freedom fighters such as Bhagat Singh, whom they branded a terrorist and sent to the gallows. The title of the 1935 Prabhat film

---

[1] Sacred scriptures: the basis of Hinduism.
[2] Phalke's definition of a *Swadeshi* film is one made by Indians with Indian capital, technicians, know-how and subject matter. The only resources he could not obtain in India were the raw stock and equipment, such as cameras, which could not be manufactured locally.
[3] The dominant genre of early Hindi films.
[4] Mythological heroes from the epic Mahabharata, known for their warrior-like qualities.

[5] A native Indian who, having spent a period in England, returns to his homeland.
[6] A film genre that deals with social and interpersonal issues.
[7] *Quit India* was a mass movement started by Mahatma Gandhi in 1942 to force the British to leave India through organised demonstrations, protest rallies and non-cooperation with the administration.

Mahatma had to be changed to *Dharmatma*, although the film had nothing to do with the life of Mahatma Gandhi. Because the system of censorship involved multiple boards, instances of films being passed by one board and rejected by an-other were quite common. What was alright for Bombay could be treated as objectionable for Kolkata. Such were the vagaries of censorship in the Raj days.[8]

National perceptions

Ironically, there were few dramatic improvements in censorship practices after the national government took over, although their perceptions were different from the colonial government's. The five regional boards were combined into one central entity, the CBFC, under the charge of an independent chairman. Its headquarters were in Bombay, and there were local offices in the major film production centres for the convenience of regional-language film-makers. A new set of do's and don'ts were drawn up, which took national priorities into account.

Colonial taboos were reassessed and re-formulated, and some old guidelines were scrapped by the new ruling class. Blind allegiance to national and patriotic sentiments was insisted upon. Even a remote possibility of an expression of dissent or a questioning of the state or the establishment was not only frowned upon but also vehemently discouraged. And so, film-makers took the path of least resistance and toed the official line willy-nilly. No one wanted to invite the wrath of the new 'gods', and they meekly submitted to the censors' dictates. Satyajit Ray's[9] experience with the national censors is a classic case. In his *Parash Pathar* (The Philosopher's Stone, 1957), one of the characters in an evening cocktail party scene is shown wearing the familiar white *khadar* cap, or 'Gandhi cap', normally worn by congressmen. The censors objected as they felt the image of a congressman consuming alcohol in public was too sacrilegious to be shown in a public medium like cinema. The same happened to scenes showing a policeman accepting a bribe while on duty. But things have changed a lot since then, and neither this type of scene nor on-screen kissing are considered so taboo anymore.

On the other hand, it became possible to interpret without fear the glorious moments of our history and the lives and times of our national heroes and freedom fighters: Jhansi Ki Rain, Bhagat Singh, Chandrasekhar Azad, Subhaschandra Bose and other martyrs, who laid down their lives fighting against the British. This was not possible under the Raj. The Indian soldier who was portrayed more as a mercenary in the early days ultimately found his true identity as a nationalist patriot fighting for his *mathrubhoomi* (motherland). The partition and division of the country into two independent nations – India and Pakistan – and the tragedy and bitterness that followed, created mounting challenges for film-makers and for the Censor Board. The film-maker, in his eagerness to avoid any controversy or conflict with one side or the other – for he could not afford to alienate either community – tactfully transplanted the tragedy from the national to the domestic space. He showed the break up of India's traditional and deep-rooted joint family system, which people from both the north and the south could identify with. The romantic concept of a new nation and idealised nation-building activities were very much evident in the films of the immediate post-independence years. However, the honeymoon was quite short-lived and as people started losing faith in their leaders, it soon gave way to disillusionment, frustration, and creeping demoralisation. The censors had to change with the changing times.

Political censorship

Political censorship, however, did not change. The pointing of a critical finger at the ruling party or the laying bare of their acts of omission and commission was fiercely opposed. Such acts were viewed as disruptive and a threat to national security. The government is empowered to withhold a film on the basis of a claim that it could create a law-and-order problem. Unfortunately, this is merely an excuse, and more often than not the Board's power is utilised to settle scores between political and ideological opponents. In India, the Board functions as an appendage of the ruling party, and this definitely deters freedom of expression and thought. For this reason the judiciary must frequently intervene, superseding the Board and passing the film, and thereby putting the very purpose of censorship into question. So it is high time for us to take a fresh look at the way censorship has been operating in India. What is lacking is the political will to approach the subject of censorship objectively and dispassionately.

While we often pride ourselves on the principles enshrined in our enlightened constitution, which guarantees freedom of speech and freedom of expression to any Indian citizen, when it comes to cinema, our rulers – whether left, right or centre – invariably seem to have cold feet. Presumably they want to play safe. Surely, it is a sad reflection of their lack of confidence in themselves, and in turn their lack of faith in us, the people.

Censorship today

A recent controversy was sparked off when the previous, Hindu-oriented, BJP government led by Prime Minister Mr. Vajpayee, banned several films and videos about the Gujarat incidents.[10] They also introduced a fresh clause in the rules governing the Mumbai International Documentary Film Festival, requiring that all Indian films and videos submitted for entry should have a censor certificate. There was a huge protest, and a boycott of the festival by some of the country's leading documentary film-makers, including Anand Patwardhan, Ranjan Palit and Rakesh Sharma. They held parallel screenings of the films denied certificates opposite the main festival venue. A fully-fledged campaign against censorship was started, and it has continued because no appreciable change has taken place even with the coming to power of the new government.

The question is this: who gives the five or six 'wise' men and women that make up the Censor Board the moral and constitutional authority to decide what sort of films their fellow citizens can and cannot see on their cinema screens? We are supposed to be a staunchly democratic nation brought up in the best democratic tradition, which teaches us to give equal respect to alternative viewpoints. Is censorship not an indication of a lack of faith in oneself and our fellow citizens? If we are intelligent enough to vote for the leader we want, why can we not be given the opportunity to select the films we want to see? When more than seventy television channels are sending images and sounds to drawing rooms around the clock and without any restriction, what is the relevance of the censorship of films screened in theatres? Apparently, some of our bureaucrats and politicians want us to believe that if censorship were to be abolished tomorrow, our country would soon be reduced to a decadent nation inhabited by immoral goons, sadistic killers and terrorists. And so they have become the self-appointed watchdogs of society. These and other issues keep haunting me whenever I think of film censorship in this country.

---

[8] *Raj* is used to describe the period of British rule. The literal translation of *Raj* is 'King'.
[9] Satyajit Ray, who made films in Bengali, is one of the best known Indian film-makers abroad. The maker of many classic films including *Pathar Panchali*, *Jalsaghar*, *Mahanagar*, and *Charulata*, he won an Oscar for his complete oeuvre.
[10] During 2000 and 2003, several violent incidents between Muslims and Hindus shocked the country.

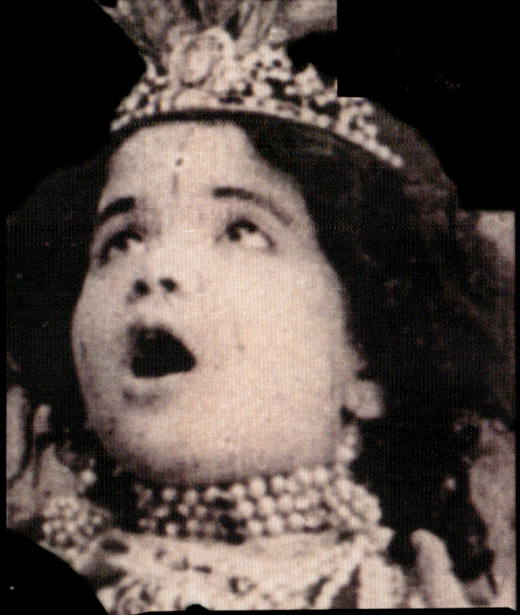

ABOVE: The young Krishna in **Kaliya Mardan** (1919)

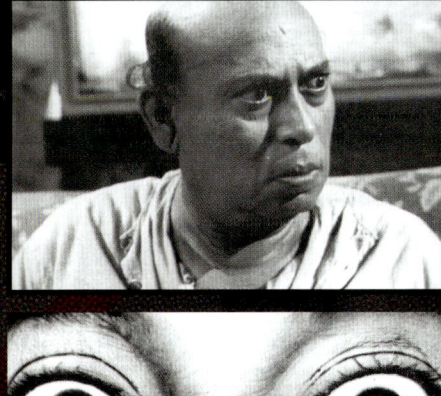

TOP: Paresh Chandra
ABOVE: **Parash Pathar** (The Philosopher's Stone, 1957)

ABOVE: **Shaheed Bhagat Singh**, advertisement (1953)

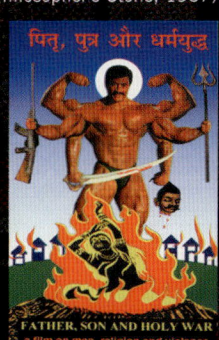

LEFT: Anand Patwardhan's **Ram Ke Naam** (In the Name of God, 1992)
RIGHT: Anand Patwardhan's **Pitru Putra aur Dharamyudh** (Father, Son and Holy War, 1994)

DEVOTION
GOD AND FAMILY

BY: DEEPA GAHLOT

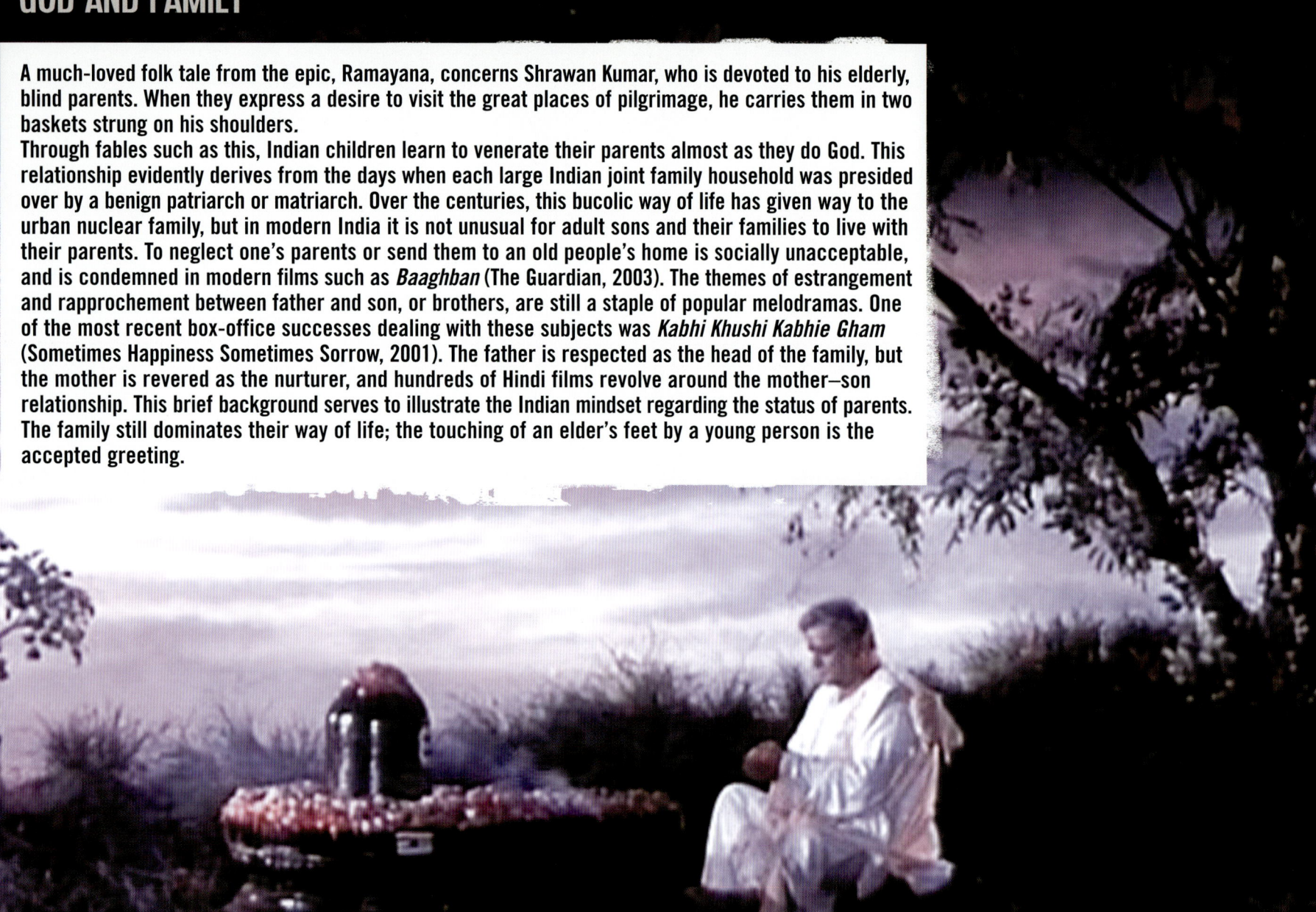

A much-loved folk tale from the epic, Ramayana, concerns Shrawan Kumar, who is devoted to his elderly, blind parents. When they express a desire to visit the great places of pilgrimage, he carries them in two baskets strung on his shoulders.

Through fables such as this, Indian children learn to venerate their parents almost as they do God. This relationship evidently derives from the days when each large Indian joint family household was presided over by a benign patriarch or matriarch. Over the centuries, this bucolic way of life has given way to the urban nuclear family, but in modern India it is not unusual for adult sons and their families to live with their parents. To neglect one's parents or send them to an old people's home is socially unacceptable, and is condemned in modern films such as *Baaghban* (The Guardian, 2003). The themes of estrangement and rapprochement between father and son, or brothers, are still a staple of popular melodramas. One of the most recent box-office successes dealing with these subjects was *Kabhi Khushi Kabhie Gham* (Sometimes Happiness Sometimes Sorrow, 2001). The father is respected as the head of the family, but the mother is revered as the nurturer, and hundreds of Hindi films revolve around the mother–son relationship. This brief background serves to illustrate the Indian mindset regarding the status of parents. The family still dominates their way of life; the touching of an elder's feet by a young person is the accepted greeting.

Prithviraj Kapoor praying in front of a Shiva *lingam* (phallus).

The most famous Indian film dynasty: the Kapoors

... my grandparents.

Film Dynasties

A characteristic of the Indian popular film industry is its dynasties. These are created by men, and in rare cases women, passing on their acting or film-making legacy to siblings, children, and relatives.

Every film made under the RK banner, established by actor and film-maker Raj Kapoor, starts with a shot of his father, Prithviraj Kapoor, offering prayers. This is followed by the RK logo. In the 1940s, Prithviraj Kapoor started what was to become one of the largest film dynasties in India. All three of his sons, Raj, Shammi and Shashi, and many of his cousins, half-brothers and various other relatives entered the film industry. Raj's three sons Randhir, Rishi and Rajeev became actors and film-makers, and Randhir's daughters Karisma and Kareena are also stars. Other branches of the family have extended by marriage into other Hindi film-industry families. The influence of the Kapoor 'clan' is one of the most powerful in the Bombay film world.

There are other director/producers who have also built dynasties by bringing relatives into the business. The Chopra, Sippy, Sagar, Mehra, Bhatt, Jain, and Ramsay families all became established in Indian cinema during the 1970s. It is unsurprising then that movies so often focus on parents.

Family Deities

It is perhaps because of the high-risk nature of their business that Indian film people are more religious and superstitious than most. They often dedicate films to family deities – a concept quite alien to monotheistic Western culture.

Shiva, the Destroyer, who in his Nataraja mode could be said to be the patron of the performing arts, is the most popular deity. The Holy Hindu trinity is formed by Vishnu, the Protector; Brahma, the Creator; and Shiva.
Durga is the goddess of strength, Kali is the militant form of Durga, and Krishna (like Ram) is an incarnation of Vishnu.[1] Other deities include: Laxmi, the goddess of wealth; Saraswati, the goddess of learning; and Hanuman, or Maruti, the monkey god, a loyal devotee of Ram who was blessed and is worshipped as a deity himself. The elephant-headed Ganapati, or Ganesh, is the god of auspicious beginnings and a remover of obstacles. He is especially revered in Bombay.

That spiritualism still suffuses the air of popular cinema is demonstrated by the continued performance of the *muhurat* ritual: Before the first scene is shot, the moment is made auspicious by a *Pooja* (offering) and the breaking of a coconut. The muhurat is always performed, regardless of the religious beliefs of the film-maker, and is unique to the Indian film industry.

[1] According to mythic lore, whenever there is too much evil in the world an avatar, or incarnation, of *Vishnu* comes to earth to save mankind.

ABOVE: **Kabhi Khushi Kabhie Gham** (2001)

LEFT PAGE & ABOVE: **Kabhi Khushi Kabhie Gham** (2001)
RIGHT: Hema Malini and Amitabh Bachchan in **Baaghban** (2003)

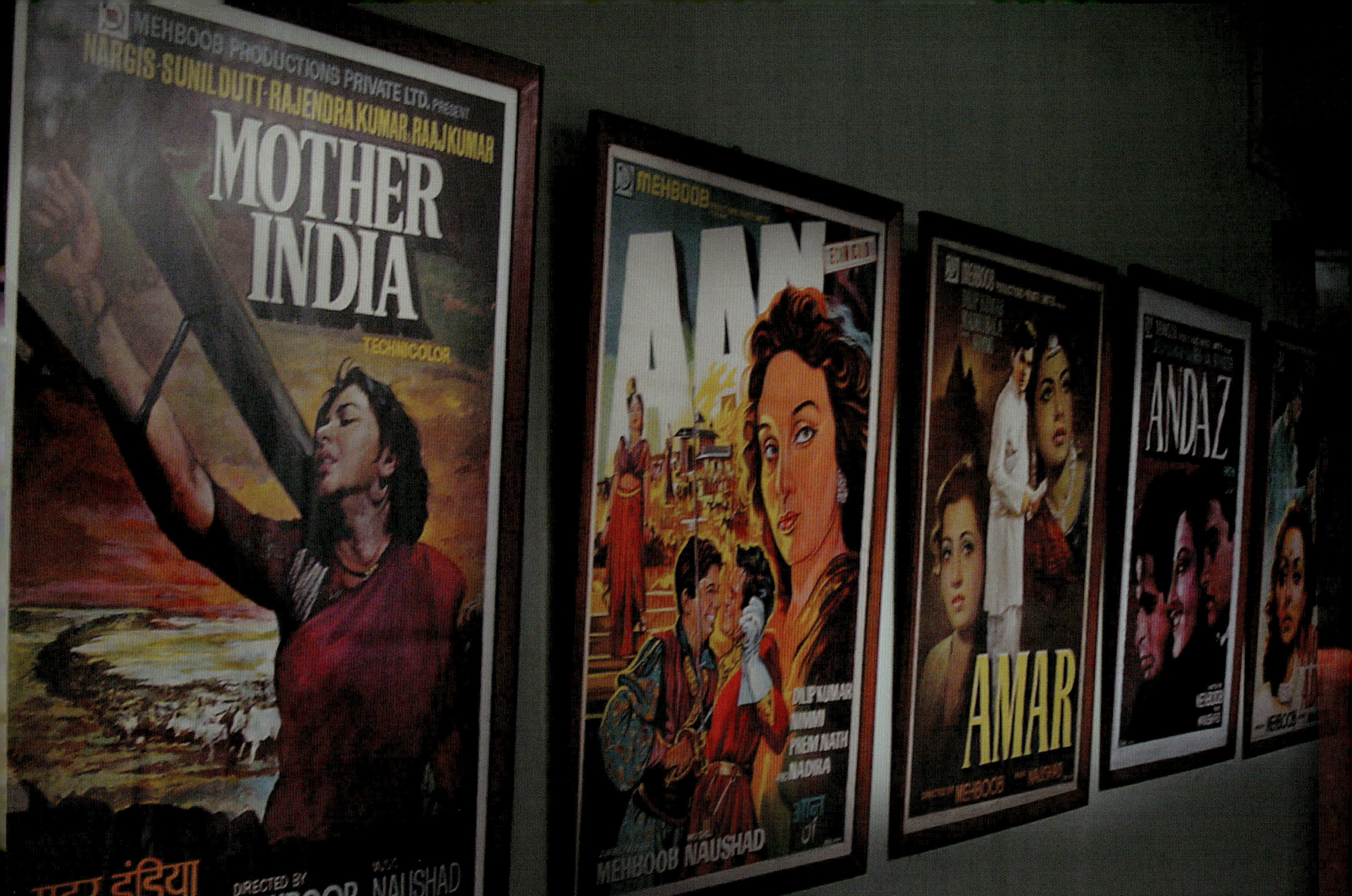

Mehboob Khan's 'Hall of Fame'

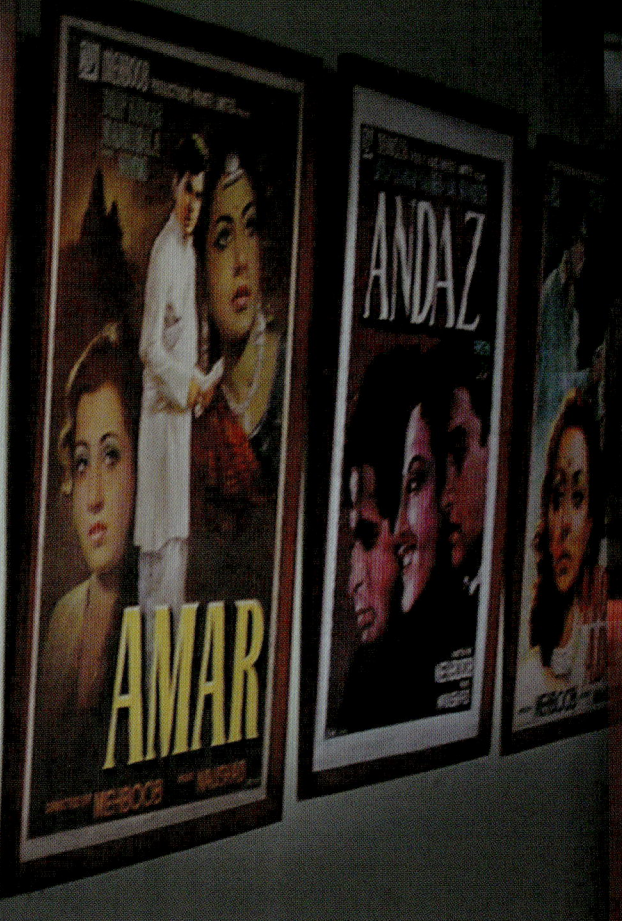

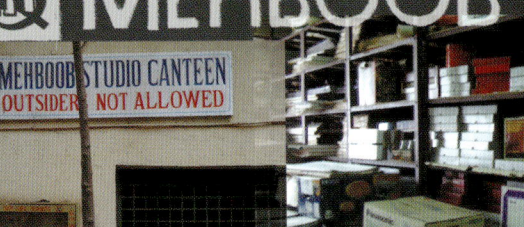

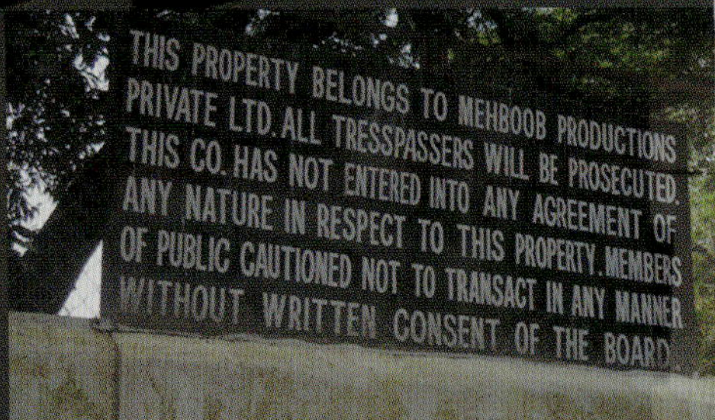

MEHBOOB

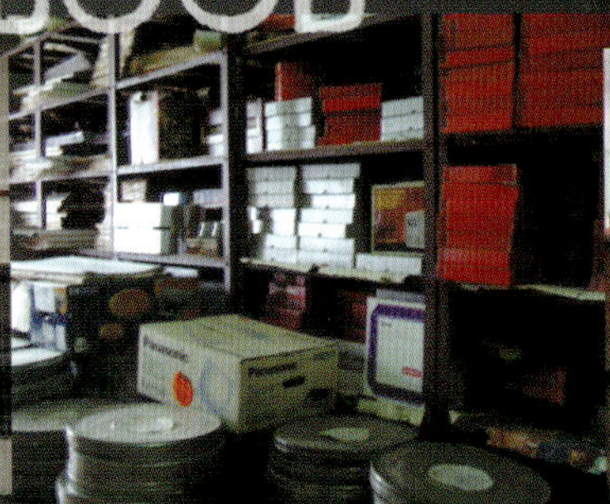

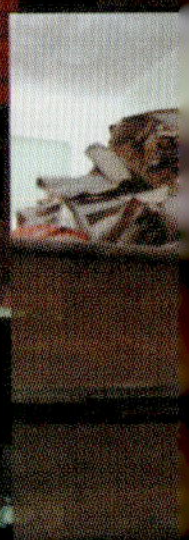

PRODUCTION BANNERS
BY: DEEPA GAHLOT

1 JJ Films:
Fire is an important symbol in banners and on posters. Flames (*sholay*) or fire (*agni*) feature in numerous films titles and on many posters. Fire is one of the oldest powers; it is both a symbol for destruction and a requirement for the creation of new life.

2 Pramod Films:
Shiva in dance pose (*nrityamurti*). Dance is the universal act of creation. Shiva is standing on a lotus pedestal.

3 PMP films:
Halo of leaves or flames (*prabhamandala*). The holy tree symbolises cosmic power.

4 Trimurti films:
Trimurti is the name of the syncretistic composition of the Hindu Triad, the holiest Hindu trinity – the gods Brahma, Vishnu and Shiva. Shiva's trident (*trishula*) symbolises him as creator, protector and destroyer. The trident is a magical weapon against demons.

The *chakra* is the sun wheel, the symbol for the circle of life and death. Vishnu can also use it as a weapon. The triangle, pointing upwards, symbolises male energy, as do the spearhead and flame; all are representations of the phallus (*lingam*).

5 Mukta Arts:
Within the headphones is the sacred *Om* sign. *Om* is the holiest mantra, a basic sound: the beginning of creation.

6 PP Prasad:
Sarasvati, the goddess of science, poetry and music, portrayed with the Indian lute (*vina*) reclining on the company's initials.

7 Sagar Art International:
The halo of flames represents cosmic power. A kink horn, or conch shell (*sankha*), and a lotus blossom (*padma*) are depicted inside the halo. The shell is used as a musical instrument, and the sound it produces is a weapon against demons.

Indian film production companies and studios, or 'banners', tend not to have unconventional names comparable to the American *Dog Eat Dog Films*, or evocative ones such as *Dreamworks* or *Castle Rock*. They usually relate to the names of their owners – producers who have rather sober attitudes to their business identities. Examples of such companies are Raj Kapoor's *RK Films*, Yash Chopra's *Yashraj Films*, BR Chopra's *BR Films*, Ramgopal Varma's *Varma Corp*, Amitabh Bachchan's *AB Corp*, Pritish Nandy Communications (PNC), Aamir Khan Productions, Devgan Entertainment and so on.

From the birth of Indian film with *Raja Harishchandra* (King Harishchandra) made by Dadasaheb Phalke's *Phalke Films* in 1913, most early banners were named after their owners. This is also true for *Madan Pictures* and *Wadia Movietone*, which were established in the 1930s. Some wished to suggest loftier associations with grand names such as *Imperial Movietone*, *Kohinoor* and *Taj Mahal*, while others preferred the more prosaic *Indo-British Film Company*, *Oriental*, *Young India* or *New Theatres*.

Some production houses derived their names from their location, such as *Bombay Talkies*, and some, *Filmistan* and *Filmalaya*, involved limited wordplay, while *Prabhat* (Dawn) and *Sagar* (Ocean) were inspired by nature.

Major film-makers of the 1950s, including Mehboob, Guru Dutt and Bimal Roy, also included their names in their banners. A generation later, while the Sippys, Manmohan Desai and Prakash Mehra continued this tradition, several used family members' names: *Navketan* is named after Dev Anand's cousin Ketan; Subhash Ghai's *Mukta Arts* after his wife; Vashu Bhagnani's *Pooja Films* after his daughter; and Pahlaj Nihalani's *Chiragdeep* after his son.

Some banners whose appellations are not derived from personal names are: *Shringar Films*, named for the *Rasa*, the mood associated with romance; The Bhatts' banner *Vishesh*, meaning 'Special'; and Yash Johar's *Dharma Productions*, which recalls his sentimental attachment to the film that set him on the path of independent production, *Dharma*.

Some film companies are named after religious deities. Examples are: *Shivam Chitrya* (Shiva) *Maruti International* (Hanuman/Maruti), *Saraswati Audiovisuals* (Saraswati) and *Ashtavinayak Films* (Ganapati/Vinayak). *Trishakti Films* is named after the goddess Durga who is also known as Shakti (strength). Tirupati and Balaji, names for Lord Krishna, have also been used.

In general, superstition, vanity, or astrologers' advice rather than wit or imagination informs the naming of production houses. Only recently have some younger producers found names that are neither self-referential nor religious. Shahrukh Khan and his associates named one banner *Dreamz*, and later another the brash *Red Chillies Films*. Ritesh Sidhwani and Farhan Akhtar called their company *Excel* and Govind Nihalani's production house is *Udbhav Dreamzone*.

In a rare combination of humour and honesty, Ramgopal Varma, accused of churning out films as if from a conveyor belt, calls his office *The Factory* and his films 'Factory products'.

SILENCE P

Mehboob's film studio

CREDITS

BY: DEEPA GAHLOT

Popular Hindi cinema, inspired by the epics and folk theatre, works within set parameters. If a mainstream or commercial film does not have songs, dances, romance and familiar relationship patterns, it is considered an exception to the rule. In keeping with oft-repeated story lines, formulaic elements and audience expectations, characters in most popular films fall within broad stereotypes.

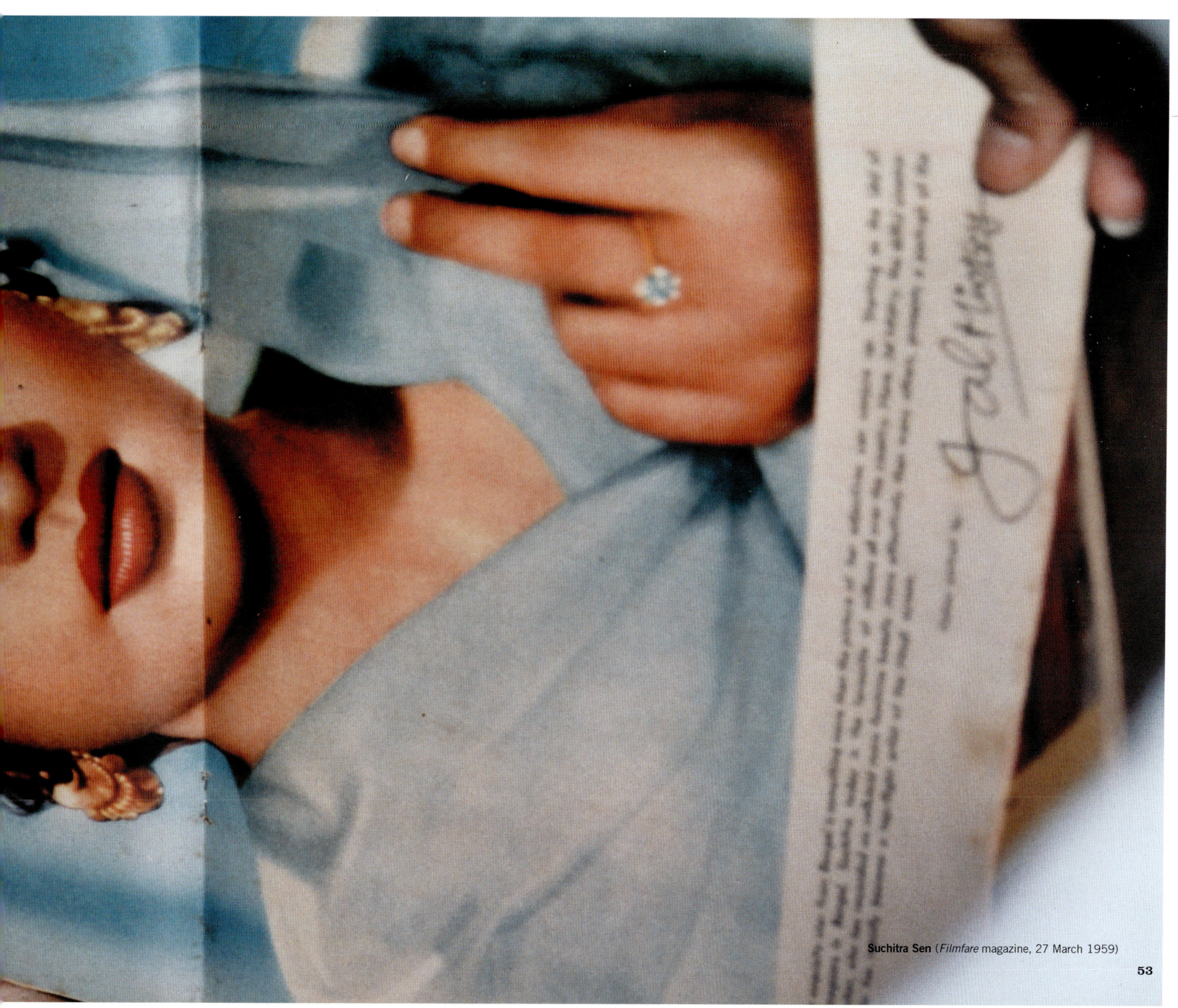

Suchitra Sen (*Filmfare* magazine, 27 March 1959)

Raj Kapoor (Sangam)

Dilip Kumar (Mughal-E-Azam)

SHAMMI KAPOOR (Kashmir Ki Kali)

Dev Anand (Swami Dada)

Rishi K

Ashok Kumar

Manoj Bajpai

Vivek Oberoi

AMITABH BACHCHAN

Salman Khan

Ajay Devgan

HRITHIK ROSHAN – Kabhi Khushi Kabhie Gham

Dharmendra (Yaane Dushman)

Guru

Saif Ali

Aamir Khan (Lagaan)

SHAH RUKH KH

The Hero

The hero is usually an epitome of goodness, strength and noble values. He is the perfect son, brother, boyfriend or husband. He fights the evil villain and always emerges victorious. The image of the hero may have changed from the soft romantic to action-oriented avenging angel, but he is invariably larger than life. Leading men playing heroes go on to exert a major influence on young men of their generation, whether it is the sensitive romantic (Dilip Kumar, Raj Kapoor, Rakesh Khanna), the rebel (Shammi Kapoor), the angry young man (Amitabh Bachchan), or the dancing swain (Rishi Kapoor, Govinda). The hero's appearance has changed from soft and poetic, to robust, to the muscular style of the contemporary leading man. Occasionally, he takes on the dark shades of the anti-hero, and for a short period in the 1990s the gangster was a popular hero. However, since the return of romance and family values to films, current leading men like Shah Rukh Khan and Hrithik Roshan uphold the popular definition of the hero as a glamourised version of the boy-next-door.

The Heroine

For many years, the heroine in Hindi films was expected to be the virginal, submissive foil to the righteous hero. She demurely accepted his romantic overtures, supported him as his beloved or wife, suffered for the sake of the family's happiness, and played the part of unblemished *devi* (goddess) to the hilt. Occasionally, she becomes *shakti* (strength) when provoked beyond the level of tolerance, but the avenging heroine is still a rarity. When Hindi cinema went through a phase of producing predominantly action films in the Amitabh Bachchan period, from the 1970s until the early 1990s, the heroine was no more than a glamorous showpiece. The heroine is almost always fair-skinned, wide-eyed and long-haired – the voluptuous *nayika* (heroine) of ancient sculpture and folk art. It is only in some recent films that the heroine has been permitted a predatory sexual identity. Today, the heroine is dressed in sexy Western clothes, has acquired an occasionally strident voice, and has dropped the virginal demeanour that was *de rigueur* for the heroine of yore. Examples of these modern heroines are Bipasha Basu in *Jism* (The Body, 2003), Mallika Sherawat in *Murder* (2004), Meghna Naidu in *Hawas* (Desire, 2004) and Kareena Kapoor in *Fida* (Devotion, 2004). So far, these changes seem only cosmetic; the gains of the women's emancipation movement have not affected the Hindi film heroine at a deeper spiritual level. She may dress like an American pop idol, but at heart she wants the status quo of love, marriage and family.

Zeenat Aman

Aishwarya Rai

Meena Kumari

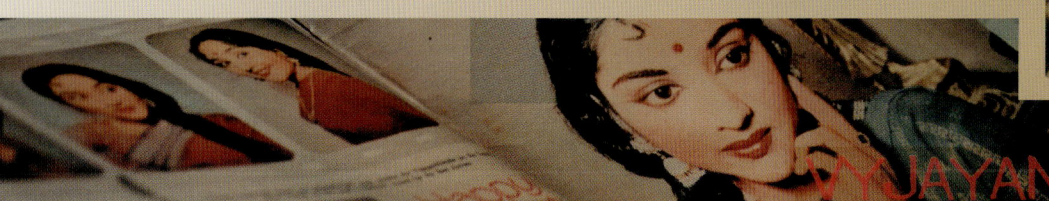

Manisha Koirala | Kajol | Tabu

Preity Zinta

Karisma Kapoor

Madhuri Dixit

Pran (Chandi Sona)

Pran (Aap Ke Diwane)

PRAN (Amar Akbar Anthony)

Pran (Jonny Mera Naam)

Danny Dengzongpa

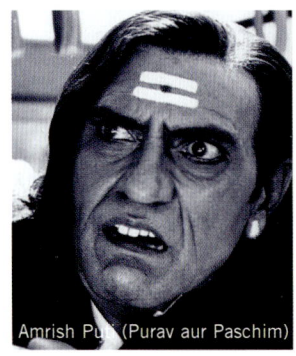
Pran (Purav aur Paschim)

Prem Chopra (Hare Rama Hare Krishna)

Yakub

Jeevan

Amrish Puri (Purav aur Paschim)

AMRISH PURI (Akhiri Intaqam)

Gulshan Grover (Saudagar)

Ranjeet (Amar Akbar Anthony)

The Villain

In the simplified universe of the Hindi film, the villain represents the forces of evil that will ultimately be vanquished by the hero, ensuring that righteousness prevails. However, as film plots have moved from the bucolic to the urban, the villain has also undergone transformations: from cruel landlord to smuggler to terrorist to corrupt politician to gangster – a rapidly changing rogues' gallery. The nature of the villain has changed far more drastically than that of the hero. He has been upgraded to the epitome of evil whether he is the bad man molesting the heroine or the international crime boss threatening the nation. This type of character holds such fascination that almost all contemporary leading men have at least one such role to their credit. K.N. Singh, Kanhaiyalal, Pran, Prem Chopra, Ranjit, Amrish Puri, Shakti Kapoor, Amjad Khan, Danny Denzongpa and Gulshan Grover are all famous villains.

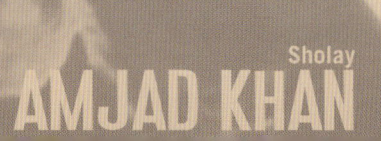
AMJAD KHAN *Sholay*

Bindu (Hawas)

Bindu (Hawas)

Bindu (Chuppa Rustam)

(Hum Hindustani)

HELEN (Hum Hindustani)

BINDU

Bindu (Zanjeer)

Dayamat Ishaa

Isha Koppikar

Isha Koppikar

Mother-in-Law, Courtesan and Vamp

The range of evil that can be expressed by female characters is far more limited than that of the male villain. Since women in traditional Indian families were confined to the home, the female embodiment of evil was the mother-in-law torturing her hapless daughter-in-law, the stepmother unleashing cruelty on her stepchildren, or the snooty daughter-in-law conspiring to break up the happy joint family. Then there was the seductress outside the home – the courtesan, the cabaret dancer or the moll – whose unbridled sexuality threatened the placid social order that has the family at its core. The man strayed and returned home duly chastened. Occasionally, the courtesan redeemed herself by sacrificing her own life to save the hero. The one change that time has wrought on the portrayal of women in Hindi films is that a vamp is no longer needed to provide the sexual heat, as it were; the modern heroine is quite willing to show a lot of skin. Best known of the actresses who have played vamps and courtesans in Hindi cinema are Cuckoo, Helen, Shashikala, Bindu and Ishaa Koppikar.

A mother of India shot her own evil son with her own hand so that the good ones may carry the flame of life from one to another in love & harmony......

WITH SPIRIT GREATER THAN FLESH SHE MADE SACRIFICE THE SUPREME — SYMBOL OF MOTHERHOOD!

Booklet **Mother India** (1957)

SCREEN'S "GODDESS" NIRUPA ROY IS SIMPLICITY PERSONIFIED

The Mother

In a predominantly patriarchal society that gives women so little power, a mother of sons is definitely at the pinnacle of the female hierarchy. The mother has considerable control over her children. This is especially true of the widowed mother character in many popular Hindi films who makes immense sacrifices to raise her children – epitomised by Nargis in Mehboob Khan's *Mother India* (1957). In return, she earns their gratitude and veneration. But if the mother character does not have much importance in the plot she is merely the submissive woman who stands by her husband no matter what. It is unsurprising, then, that the one enduring classic of Hindi cinema is *Mother India*, in which a strong and virtuous widow single-handedly raises her children in excruciatingly impecunious circumstances, but nonetheless picks up a gun to kill her outlaw son. It is an extreme sacrifice indeed, when a woman puts the good of society before her own family. Famous 'mothers' are Leela Chitnis, Achala Sachdev, Lalita Pawar, Leela Mishra, Durga Khote and Nirupa Roy.

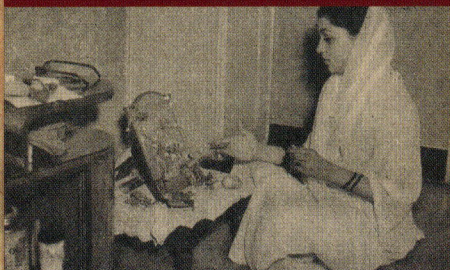

I'm here... Your mother.
Nirupa Roy (Deewaar)

Durga Khote (Mughal-e-Azam)

Jaya Bachchan (Kabhi Khushi Kabhie Gham)

# Bimal Roy Productions

Yash Chopra's

 Directed By **Manmohan Desai**

The Director

By rights the director should be in the commanding seat, but in the world of commercial Hindi film, directors are confronted with too many obstacles to realise their visions without making any compromises. The star is clearly the most important factor in the making and marketing of a film, and the director often has to work under several constraints. It has been years since Hindi mainstream cinema has seen a true auteur such as Raj Kapoor, Guru Dutt, Bimal Roy or Shantaram. The one notable exception is Mani Ratnam, who has influenced Bombay Hindi cinema even though he mostly works in Tamil. He chooses original subjects and has developed a unique style.

Filmed By R.K Films **Raj Kapoor**

 # Karan Johar

 # Sanjay Leela Bhansali

Mani Ratnam

story · screenplay · dialogue

The Scriptwriter
In Hollywood, the writer is an important part of the film-making process: a novelist may receive millions of dollars for the movie rights to a book, and a scriptwriter is paid to develop an original or adapted screenplay. The Bombay film industry treats the writer as a lowly hack. More often than not, the producer wants to copy a foreign film, in which case the writer simply 'Indianises' the names and situations, and passes off the work as his own. Frequently, scenes and lines are written on the set, and often changed to suit a star's mood. Writers complain that original screenplays are mangled beyond recognition by the director, the producer, the star and even the distributor – each of whom might want to include elements that appeal to a mass audience. This disrespect for intellectual property is apparent in the poor quality of most commercial films. Scriptwriters who have made names for themselves are Wajahat Mirza, Akhtar Mirza, KA Abbas, Sachin Bhowmik, Prayag Raj and Salim-Javed.

CHOREOGRAPHY

dances

Farah Khan

Saroj Khan

The Choreographer
Because songs and dances are integral to popular Hindi film, the choreographer is an important member of the film crew – even more so of late, because lavishly *picturised* (visualised) songs have become promotional tools for films. In the old days, song picturisation was simple and in keeping with the tone of the film, and a choreographer was only required for a formal classical or folk-dance number. Then came the trend of unrealistic song sequences in which the hero and heroine sang romantic songs with dozens of extras dancing in the background. Also, ever since television promos became crucial to publicising films, there has been a demand for extravagantly-shot song and dance sequences – whether needed in the films or not. For example, a seductive dance number is added to the film, though it is not part of the narrative structure. It is then up to the choreographer, or dance director, to come up with imaginative dance movements – and to film them well too. It is common in the Bombay industry for the director not to be present when the song scenes are shot, because this is the choreographer's job. The early choreographers – Satyanarayan, Suresh Bhatt, Kamal, Madhav Krishna – were all men, but nowadays women such as Farah Khan and Saroj Khan are among the most famous dance directors.

PLAY BACK SINGERS

Asha Bhosle

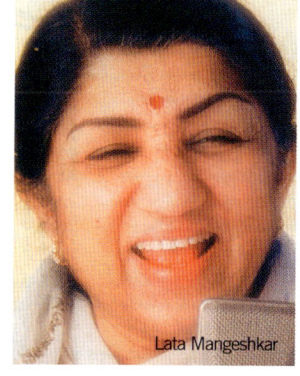
Lata Mangeshkar

Udit Narayan

Sonu Nigam

The Playback Singer
When sound was introduced into Hindi films with the first talkie, *Alam Ara* (The Light of the World, 1931), the actors had to sing 'live'. Many actors lost their jobs because they could not sing, but those who could, like K.L Saigal and Kanan Devi, were the stars of the day. The system of playback singing, or miming, was introduced in 1935, and involves actors lip-synching to songs pre-recorded in a studio. Because popular songs contributed to a film's success, playback singers became stars in their own right, and had their own fan followings. Lata Mangeshkar, Mohammad Rafi, Mukesh, Asha Bhosle, and Kishore Kumar were the trendsetters, and their style is still imitated by contemporary singers such as Shaan, Alka Yagnik, Kavita Krishnamurthy, Udit Narayan, Sonu Nigam and Sunidhi Chauhan.

R.D. Burman

Rajesh Roshan

Anu Malik

A.R. Rehman

The Composer

Film music changed from classical and folk-based songs to tunes inspired by rock and pop in post-1970s cinema. For a while, noisy pop and disco imitations ruled, and melody was forgotten in Hindi cinema. Today's young listeners want music they can dance to, and contemporary composers have adapted, plagiarised, remixed and innovated to create a more urban, international sound for film songs. The music composer's clout varies according to the state of music at any given time; if his albums sell, the composer is king. Piracy has almost killed the film music market in modern times and, with a couple of notable exceptions, the composer comes considerably lower in the film industry pecking order than once was the case. The composers Naushad, SD Burman, Shankar Jaikishen, Roshan, Madan Mohan, RD Burman and Laxmikant Pyarelal were the trendsetters in the fifties and sixties; the modern composers Anu Malik, AR Rahman and others have a great tradition to live up to.

The Lyricist

During the golden age of Hindi cinema in the 1950s, famous poets such as Sahir Ludhianvi, Majrooh Sultanpuri and Kaifi Azmi were drawn to cinema, and wrote beautiful songs that fitted into the narratives of films. In the 1970s, action films came into vogue and they were soon followed by the disco boom. The importance of the lyricist was eroded because songs were not expected to express delicate or poetic emotions. Contemporary film music is a mix of the lyrical and the pedestrian, but the age of poetry in film is dead. However, lyricists such as Gulzar and Javed Akhtar and others have saved film song from deteriorating into unintelligibility.

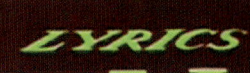

Sameer

Javed Akhtar

Kaifi Azmi & Shabana Azmi

Gulzar

The Song and Dance Sequence

Besides following the structure of folk theatre, in which song and dance interludes were part of the package, the popular Hindi film needs its song and dance sequences for various reasons. Primary among them is that music is part of an Indian culture that has songs for births, marriages, festivals and other celebrations. Several Indian festivals, including *Holi*, *Baisakhi*, and *Navratri*, are accompanied by dancing. The vigorous *Bhangra* (folk music) of Punjab and the *Raas-Garba-Dandiya* (dance with sticks) of Gujarat, have now crossed regional boundaries and attained national popularity. There was no way that films could escape the influence of music. The great pioneering directors integrated songs into the story and used them to propel the narrative. They conveyed, with economy and emotion, what it might have taken several scenes and much dialogue to express with equal power. The song sequence also offers relief if the film has too many heavy or tragic moments. Since all Hindi films have a romantic thematic element, what better way to portray love between the hero and heroine than a well-worded song? Today a snazzily picturised song and dance number is an effective marketing device and audiences often go to see a film if they like the look and sound of these scenes.

LEFT: Detail from *The Rasa Dance*
BELOW: **Raas-Garba-Dandiya** dance

ENTERTAINMENT & ESCAPISM

BY: GAYATRI CHATTERJEE

The terms *entertainment* and *escapist cinema* are particularly associated with commercial films made in Bombay, Kolkata, Chennai and elsewhere in India. Any investigation such as the following must seek out the more complex truth behind the assumption that cinema is merely entertainment and escapism.

Indian cinema can be seen as an extension of the popular performative arts that are traditionally closely associated with all aspects of social life, events and rituals. Higher castes were not permitted to join the performing professions, which were the domain of the artisan classes, who were marginalised. They nonetheless gained an important position in the community due to the social significance of ritual and their art. A similar paradox applies to film, which is considered beneficial as well as harmful to society. If cinema, the pre-eminent modern performance medium, is regarded with disapproval, then something is obviously in need of investigation.

From its inception, practitioners and the public alike have regarded cinema with extreme passion as well as suspicion. National leaders, Mahatma Gandhi in particular, were suspicious, or even contemptuous of it and of film actors who engaged in local and national politics. Others used it as a medium for winning over the masses, while middle-class intellectuals recognised its potential for self-expression and shaping the modern Indian.

Many films bear witness to this ambivalence towards the medium. In *Street Singer* (1938), the hero and heroine come to Calcutta to earn their living and are picked up by a film company. Ultimately, they become disillusioned with the film industry, leave the city and return to their former lives as itinerant singers. The world of cinema is portrayed as one that devalues life and life's good things such as love and music.

Disappointment with the contemporary, and the desire to escape

After independence in 1947, the leader of the nation, Gandhi, wanted to establish a *ram-rajya* (reign of the god Ram) in India. He adopted a song about this epic hero to propagate and fix his ideology in the minds of the people. *Awaara* (The Vagabond,1951) is explicit in its criticism of the newly formed nation-state. The hero's father is depicted as a heartless patriarch, named after Ram. Raj, the hero played by the film's director Raj Kapoor, leads a life of crime in a hellish world that his father has created; he sings 'I do not want this hell; I want flowers, songs, love and the spring.' Many post-independence films depict modern urban India as hell; they often try to find ways of escape, and strive to create a paradise for its principal protagonists. *Awaara* ends with Raj going to jail, hoping that after release he will occupy top administrative and legal positions like his father. Some films resolve these issues with compromises, while others speak of leaving this world forever – actually or metaphorically.

ABOVE: **Awaara** (1951)

In *Daag* (Stigma, 1952), the main character, Dilip Kumar, is a poor man from a small town who, lacking opportunities in life, takes to drink. He sings the popular song *Ai mere dil kahin aur chal* (O my heart, let us go away somewhere!). The heroine, played by Nimmi, eventually manages to rid him – and by extension the entire nation – of the evil of drink. Cleansed of alcoholism, the village becomes the utopia the heroine strove for. The film ends with the classic image of the hero and heroine running towards the horizon, but in this case, they are chasing the last drunkard away. This is an example of the kind of narrative closure that typifies mainstream cinema, making audiences happy with the impression of a perfect solution.

Disappointment with contemporary India and its leaders is expressed more darkly in *Pyaasa* (Eternal Thirst, 1957), in which the hero inquires in song 'Where are those who once had pride in this land?' The film ends with the poet-hero, played by director Guru Dutt, failed and socially marginalised, walking towards the horizon with a prostitute – that perennial marginal figure – played by Waheeda Rehman. The implication is that it is always possible to turn away from this world and leave it.

Tragic films tend to portray heroes or heroines – and sometimes their close friends or parents – as the only good people, and thus set apart from the rest of humanity. The remaining characters compare poorly with the main protagonists, aligning audience identification with the main characters.

Songs fulfil important discursive functions in traditional art forms and in films. So it is ironic that the representation of songs – accompanied by dance in films – is the main reason that cinema in India is considered 'entertainment'. Of course, there are other factors that make Indian films attractive to many and unappealing to others: displays of opulence, repeated use of coincidence and improbable events, and all manner of excess.

Above all, mainstream cinema's escapism lies in its maintenance of the status quo and its ultimate support for issues that it initially set out to define and criticise. Critical audiences see these films as failing to properly analyse the social issues and problems they raise, and teaching audiences how best to adjust and compromise.

ABOVE: **Daag** (1952)

'If entertainment and escapism reflect a desire for pleasu then Indian films portray childhood as the most importa

ABOVE & LEFT: **Pyaasa** (1957)

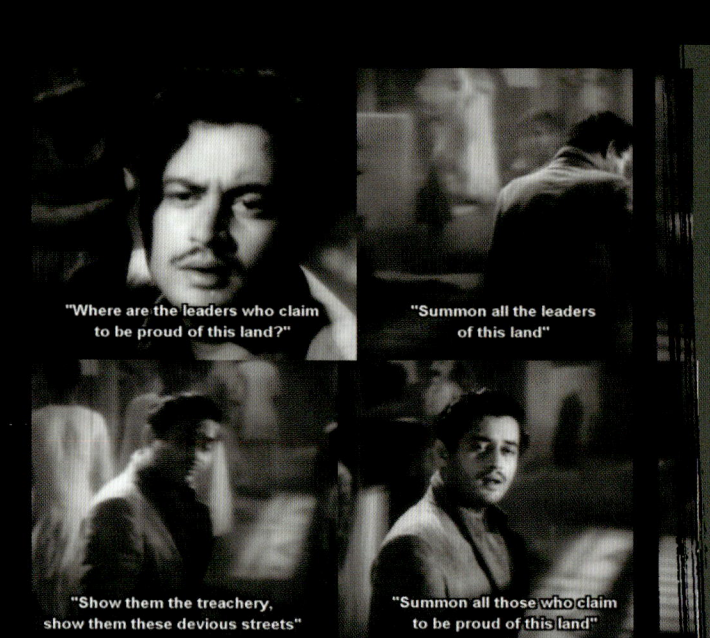
"Where are the leaders who claim to be proud of this land?"
"Summon all the leaders of this land"
"Show them the treachery, show them these devious streets"
"Summon all those who claim to be proud of this land"

Devdas (1955)

'd happiness, pository of perfect happiness'

Devdas (1935 & 2002)

Paradise lost and regained

If entertainment and escapism reflect a wish for pleasure and happiness, then Indian films portray childhood as the most important repository of perfect happiness, a golden age to be regained – now or in a possible future. Childhood friendship is a recurrent theme in films of all regions and periods, and the world of childhood is the paradise, or source, from which the protagonists fall.[1]

A concept of paradise or a utopian vision is evident in most films, and it goes without saying that love, goodness and happiness are central to them. The archetypical film *Devdas* (Devdas, 1935) is seen as having pioneered this trend, and *Aag* (Fire,1948) as having made an important contribution to its maturation. Both films begin with the separation of childhood sweethearts who must then find each other and establish the *pyaar ki duniya* (world-of-love) for themselves.

Many Indian films revolve around a dystopia, usually the city, or the desire or nostalgia for a utopia – the village. Either theme can be employed to create entertaining films for mass audiences. Although the dystopian form reflects contemporary situations, the dark sides of the city, they also often end with the hero defeating the bad guys. These films about the big bad city often set trends for street behaviour and among members of the underground. The second genre, films with pastoral themes, delineate utopia only to reveal cracks and fissures therein. But some early films, pure comedies, were dedicated to depicting the euphoria of early city formation and the joys of migration to the big city. Good or bad, the city is where men and women can meet freely and exchange emotions. Some of the many important films of this genre were made by Nasir Hussain, for example *Dil Deke Dekho* (Give Me Your Heart, 1959). These fims feature actors such as: Shammi Kapoor, whose wild dances and pelvic thrusts were likened by some to Elvis Presley's; Dev Anand whose characters were suave and urbane, and defied rules and regulations set up by family and state; and Kishor Kumar, a gifted singer, actor and director, who could create crazy situations and moods with gaiety and élan.

Love creates a paradisiacal world that audiences enter and temporarily inhabit. The film screen becomes a landscape of the faces and figures of the stars. Their physical beauty, specific gestures and mannerisms consolidate the elements of entertainment and escapism. Heroes and heroines become childlike, and sometimes even child*ish*, as they fall in love, talk, and sing and dance. Songs and dances are generally performed in beautiful landscapes.

For several decades, Bombay film-makers shot love scenes in Kashmir, known as 'paradise of the earth' since the Mughal period (1526–1760). In films such as *Junglee* (The Savage,1961), heroes went there to fall in love with the beautiful women, who were considered more innocent and sweet-natured than city girls. That these films were shot in colour was crucial; it contributed to the sense of plenitude and pleasure.

Nasir Hussain took his young protagonists to various hill stations,[2] where, away from societal and parental vigilance, they were free to have fun, express love – and 'rock ''n' roll'. Paradises are also rendered in dream sequences in elaborate Hollywood-style sets. The presence of a number of male and female friends on such occasions, which would not normally be experienced within family-dominated social structures, is an elaboration of this paradise-on-earth. Seen differently, the crowded song and dance sequences prove the couple's ability to gather a small community around them. Thus empowered, they are better able to take on and defy the world.

Bombay films portray tribal people and their settlements as the repositories of civilisation's early innocence, and *Roti* (Bread,1942) contains one of the most important representations of an Indian Shangri-la. The avaricious industrialist star of this film does not belong there of course, and dies in a desert, clutching the gold stolen from his city associates and other people.

Love in Tokyo (1966)

Kashmir Ki Kali (1964)

New utopia

The nature of the paradise or utopia presented in modern productions is changing. To a great extent they undermine the romantic modernist trend of earlier films whereby the individual was endowed with freedom and powers of self-determination. More recent films prioritise the relationships within and between families. Every aspect of family life can be entertaining; if one set of parents is evil, they are (or one of them is) amusingly so, as in *Dil* (The Heart, 1990). Actor pairs, such as Kader Khan and Govinda, who starred in *Raja Babu* (King Babu, 1994) and other productions, create a world of father–son camaraderie, and both can be equally good or equally crooked in a utopian post-Oedipal world. As entertainment, films with conspicuous and sometimes indecent displays of wealth, glamour and sexually explicit gestures, reflect the hesitance of India's entry into an age of rampant consumerism and the global market economy. Some popular modern films play on feelings of insecurity and false pride, and present virulent nationalism and jingoism as entertainment.

From the 1960s, foreign locations became increasingly popular settings for narration or song and dance scenes, for example in *Sangam* (Confluence, 1964) or *An Evening In Paris* (1967). Recently, with producers receiving backing from wealthier and/or non-resident financiers, the principal protagonists and their families often travel to foreign locations (Switzerland, Canada, Australia and more recently the USA), where they demonstrate Indian 'superiority' and money-power, as in *Pardes* (In Foreign Land, 1997). An even more modern trend, in films such as *Dil Chahta Hain* (What the Heart Desires, 2003) or *Hum Tum* (Me – You, 2004), suggests a less troubled attitude to both the homeland and to foreign nations.

ABOVE & RIGHT: **HumTum** (2004)

ABOVE: **Silsila** (1981)

An Evening in Paris (1967)

ABOVE: Celebrating *Holi* in **Sholay** (1975)
BELOW: Krishna participates in *Holi* (Nurpur c. 1770–80)

Arjuna & Krishna

MYTHOLOGY & FOLKLORE

BY: MARIJKE DE VOS

Mythology in Indian cinema is usually Hindu-oriented. The two Hindu epics, Mahabharata and Ramayana, have formed the basis of all aspects of Indian culture throughout the ages, and cinema is no exception. The gods described below are omnipresent in the Indian film world. They are encountered as statues in front of cinema halls and as symbols in production logos. Images of them often precede the opening credits, and they are frequently embodied by the main protagonists in the films themselves. The gods and holy men and women are present throughout this book too. It might therefore be useful to provide a short introduction to the most important gods and goddesses of the Hindu pantheon, with descriptions of their associated symbols and attributes.

LEFT: Krishna in front of a cinema hall
ABOVE: Shiva as Nataraj, king of the dance, patron of the performing arts.

Trimurti is the name given to the syncretistic composition of the Hindu Triad, the holiest Hindu trinity, the gods Brahma, Vishnu and Shiva. They are depicted as three heads on one body. Together they reflect the three aspects of the One Almighty Power: creation, protection and destruction.

1 Shiva, the Destroyer, is the god of love, creation and destruction. His symbol is the *lingam*, the male sexual organ, which in this context represents all-pervasive power and intelligent consciousness. He has five aspects: the cosmic dancer or king of the dance, Nataraja, in which form he is the patron of the performing arts; the young aesthete Dakshina or Mahayogi; the destroyer, Gajasura, Tripurantaka or Kalari; the fearsome Bhairava; and the protective and loving husband, Maheshvara. He is often depicted nude; his hair might be loose, tied in a knot on his head or hidden in a tall pointed crown. His three eyes represent the sun, the moon, and fire. His third eye is closed – when opened the fire it unleashes will destroy all creation. He generally has four arms, although in other incarnations he has up to eighteen.

Shiva has a crescent moon in his hair and snakes around his neck. He holds a trident (*trishula*) in his hands. The trident is a magical weapon against demons. Other attributes include a drum (*damaru*), symbolising the sound *Om*, the beginning of everything and a pitcher (*kamandalu*), symbol of his function as the creator of all life. He faces south (*dakshina*), where happiness comes from. He is the greatest yogi and master of music.

Shiva's cosmic dance symbolises the eternal movement of the universe. Through the rhythm of the dance the universe moves and manifests itself. The circle of flames around Shiva is energy in its purest form, but it is also the fire of cremation. The circle is the symbol of *Om*, the holy mantra. The drum in one hand symbolises the union of male and female. The fire in the other hand indicates his ability to destroy the universe. The elephant hand gesture suggests his power, and his uplifted foot symbolises liberation.

Parvati, Shiva's wife, is usually shown with him. Together they symbolise the dual nature of the Absolute. Shiva and Parvati, the loving couple, are a popular subject for painters. Their children are Skanda and Ganesh, the elephant god.

2 Brahma, the Creator, has four faces, of which only three can be seen. They symbolise the four Vedas, or holy texts, which were written between 1200 and 400 BC; the oral tradition goes back to 2000 BC. His four hands represent the four winds. Brahma sits on a lotus, the throne of the gods and symbol of eternal renewal and beauty, or on a goose, symbol of knowledge. His attributes are a vase (*kalasha*) that catches the nectar of eternal life, symbol of wisdom and immortality; a pitcher (*kamandalu*), symbolising his function as creator of all life; a spoon (*sruk*) with which he offers clarified butter (*ghee*), showing that even a god must make offerings; a bow (*parivati*), symbol of the death wish; a book (*pustaka*), symbol of wisdom – the written and spoken word is seen as a source for everything that exists; a lotus blossom (*padma*), for beauty, happiness and eternal renewal; a rosary (*akshamala*), which represents the cycle of everlasting time; and a sceptre (*danda*), used to punish crimes against the universal law of time.

3 Vishnu, the Protector, is often seen sitting on the snake Shesha. The snake floats on the endless ocean. Vishnu has a dark complexion, black or blue. He has four hands and wears yellow clothes. On his head he wears a tall crown. Vishnu's attributes are a war club (*gada*); a wheel (*chakra*), symbol of life and death, which is also used as weapon; a conch shell (*sankha*), a sound-weapon used against demons; and the lotus blossom, symbol for beauty, happiness, and eternal renewal. The seven heads of the snake tower above his head to protect him.

Vishnu has ten incarnations, the two best known and most frequently portrayed in the arts – especially painting, drama and cinema – are Ram and Krishna.

4 Sarasvati, Brahma's wife, is the four-armed goddess of knowledge, poetry and music She plays the Indian lute (*vina*) with two hands and holds a book, representing learning and knowledge, and a rosary in the others. She stands on a goose or sits on a lotus.

5 Laxmi, Vishnu's wife, is at his feet. She is the goddess of wealth and happiness. She has four hands. Two of them hold lotus blossoms, two others proffer costly gifts. She is gold in colour. She is one of the best-loved goddesses. In another incarnation, as Rama's wife Sita, she is associated with agriculture.

6 Rama is the seventh incarnation of Vishnu, and hero of the epic Ramayana. He is a young king, carries a bow, and is always accompanied by his wife Sita. Rama and Sita are the main protagonists of numerous dances, theatre plays and films. They are the perfect couple, virtuous and faithful.

7 Krishna, the Dark One, is the eighth incarnation of Vishnu. Krishna is depicted as either black- or blue-skinned. Krishna plays an important part in traditional Hindu culture, as he does in film. His story spans his birth, his upbringing by his foster-mother, Yashoda, and his death. The concept of the foster-mother is familiar to Indian cinema audiences. Her love is as great as any blood-mother's love for her son.

Famous tales tell of Krishna stealing butterballs as a young boy, and of how he played his flute and frolicked and danced with the cow-herding girls (*gopis*) on moonlit nights. His many heroic deeds included the vanquishing of the snake Kaliya.

Krishna's love for Radha is:
'A love not of the immediate but of the ultimate, not just sensual but equally spiritual, a love that transcends the limited personal ego and reaches out to the vast and unfettered consciousness; a love that has not the pleasure of the oneness, but the joy of the heart'
(from The Flute and the Lotus by Harsha Dehejia, Ahmedabad, 2002)

This *parakiya* love is distinct from marital love. It is a spiritual love between god (Krishna) and mankind (Radha). Krishna can be recognised by his pose, standing and playing the flute, with one leg crossed in fron of the other.

8 Durga. The female divine principle is known by the names *Devi*, goddess, or *Mahadevi*, great goddess. There are seven Mother goddesses. The Mother goddess is worshipped in two of her many aspects: her compassionate and her violent incarnations. Devotion to goddesses has led to a distinct religious movement focused on worship of them. The Mother goddess Devi, the protector, is worshipped especially in rural areas. One of the most important goddesses is Durga who is extremely powerful; she gives and takes life. She is the defiant protector who unleashes her destructive powers when the earth is threatened by demons.

Durga has eight arms. She sits on a lotus throne or rides a tiger or lion. Her symbols are: a trident, a sword, a snake, the conch shell, a drum, a shield, a bowl made from a skull, an arrow, a bow, a wheel, a mace (*gada*) and a pitcher. Durga is the most powerful goddess in India. The *Durga Puja*, one of the main religious festivals in India, celebrates Durga's victory over the buffalo demon.

9 Kali, the Black One, is the destructive power and the wisdom that ends all illusions. Her tongue, dripping the blood of her victims, hangs out of her mouth. She wears a necklace of human skulls (*kapalamala*) symbolising the cycle of life and death. Wife of Shiva, she overpowers him and dances on his body. Her iconography has developed from that of an emaciated monster to a healthy and beautiful girl. She is the more aggressive form of Durga and destroys even more atrocious monsters.

10 Hanuman, the Monkey God, is known from the epic Ramayana for his boundless loyalty. He was a general in Rama's army fighting Ravanna's demons, but, much later, he was elevated to godhood for his loyalty and good deeds. He has a monkey head and he carries a mace. A popular image shows him flying with a mountain landscape in one hand: during the battle between Rama and Ravana, Hanuman flew to the Himalayas to find medicinal herbs for the wounded Lakshmana, and because he did not know which herb to choose, he brought the entire mountain home. Hanuman is often depicted kneeling at the feet of Rama and Sita.

11 Ganesh, or Ganpati, has an elephant head. He is the most popular god. He is adored all over India, but especially in Maharashtra where a great temple is dedicated to him. He is seen as the god of wisdom, bearer of good fortune and remover of obstacles. His vehicle is a mouse.

With his four arms and fat belly, he is portrayed sitting on a lotus throne, dancing or riding on his mouse. He has a noose, symbolising his involvement in worldly affairs and his ability to ensnare evil and ignorance. The goad (*ankusha*) he holds would normally be used to control elephants. In his hands, it symbolises the ability to take action and to discern one's own motives and reign them in. Another of his attributes is food (*modaka*), a bowl full of sweets or fruit. He is paradox incarnate – he obviously enjoys both the good life and his lofty yogic principles, and thus manages to combine his enjoyment of earthly existence with deep spiritual insight. His body has the shape of the holiest mantra, *Om*.

7

8

9

10 — Lakshman, 6, Sita

11

LEFT: *Pachhvai*, dance with the sticks: a traditional folk dance
BELOW: The same dance performed in **Lagaan**.

Take my fair body and
Give me your darkness
I would lose myself in the night
And become one with my beloved
(Song from **Bandini**, 1963)

RADHA-KRISHNA LOST IN LOVE
BY: FAREEDA

The romantic pairing of Radha and Krishna is implied in the narratives of popular films through song, dance, dialogue or visual references. We are often told that the hero and heroine's love for each other is like that of Krishna and Radha. What does this mean?

Legend has it that Krishna was adopted into a family whose occupation was cow herding. He was not God's child, but God incarnate. The miracles and delights of the baby Krishna provide a rich anecdotal seam of mischief and cunning. The sentiments evoked are comical, maternal, awesome and erotic.

The erotic aspect really blossoms as Krishna grows up and achieves manhood. His dalliances with the *gopis* (cow-herding girls) of the village are the subject of poetry, song, dance, painting, and of course film.
At a secular level, the romance is imagined in all its sensuousness. Krishna's favourite *gopi* is Radha. Their preferred meeting place is a *panghat* (watering spot), which might be a well, a pond, a lake or riverbank.

She risks defamation by meeting him. He teases her by breaking her earthenware *gaagar* (water pitcher) and wetting her clothes. He pulls himself to her by her wrists, he teases and cajoles her, and beseeches her to give up her pride. She yields, and the love play starts again. However, in films this teasing often comes close to an alarming manhandling of the woman. Better-known examples of such scenes include Birju troubling a village belle who comes to the well in *Mother India* (1957), and Paro and Devdas meeting at the pond in *Devdas* (1955).

The lovers are associated with the element water; clouds and rain, and wind, forests and fruit-laden trees are as much part of the *mise en scène* as their glances and embraces. Radha's hair is fair, and Krishna's dark, hence the play on words in the song quoted above. They are eternal lovers, never man and wife, and the element of social transgression is central to their love. In general, however, commercial films have stayed within limits acceptable to social morality: rarely do we see an older Radha paired with a younger Krishna or even a married Radha. Nor do we see a hero assuming the feminine aspect in order to become one with the Lord – a ritual practiced by certain sects.

As a philosophical discourse, the longing of Radha for Krishna is that of the individuated soul for the Godhead who can only be glimpsed by surrendering the veil of ego – jealousy, pride, social status and so on. Logically, it follows that although Radha may be the favoured *gopi*, she is not the exclusive object of Krishna's attentions, for he is generous to every soul that aspires to unite with him. The worldly Radha, however, suffers dejection, jealousy and suspicion, for she knows that Krishna is not and cannot be hers alone. She pines for him, waits for him, remonstrates with him and sulks. This last is expressed in the song *Radha Kyun na Jale* (*Lagaan*, Land Tax, 2001). But he always charms her once more, and she 'realises'.

For those belonging to this culture, a mere hint of colour, a verse or an ambience can evoke this cosmic romance. Popular Indian cinema has added to this reservoir of the collective imagination. The rain-song scene – common to many Indian films, and traditionally associated with farewell, eroticism and changes in season – could once elicit such recollections, but it has now generally become an opportunity to showcase the female body. The lyrics of some of the most memorable film songs are based on this primal coupling of Radha and Krishna.

RIGHT: **Cheer Harana,** 1710-1720 (Rajasthan)
BELOW: The same scene played by Raj Kapoor and Vijayanthimala in **Sangam**

Devdas (1955)

Devdas (2002), meeting at the pond. 'The lovers are associated with the element water'.

Radha and Krishna meeting at night in a forest near a river (Aurangabad, India, 1650)

Yashoda Krishna (1975). Krishna and his foster mother Yashoda have inspired numerous films in which an infant loses its mother and is brought up by a loving foster mother.

RAM & SITA: THE PERFECT PAIR
BY: FAREEDA

If the Radha–Krishna affair is one of social transgression, the Rama –Sita pairing is one of dutiful obedience to mores and tradition. Ram is the ideal son, husband, brother or king. He is nobility incarnate, epitomising self-sacrifice and righteousness.

Ram was the eldest son of King Dashrat of Ayodhya. Dashrat had two wives. Because of a promise made to one of the queens, Dashrat was forced to abdicate in favour of his younger son Bharat and ask Rama, the heir apparent, to relinquish his right to the throne and seek refuge in the forests with his wife Sita. Here they lived for fourteen years. The epic, Ramayana, tells of Ram and Sita's journey and consequent tribulations and triumphs: Sita is abducted by Ravana who holds her captive for some time. She is rescued by Ram and his faithful allies, including an army of monkeys led by the monkey god Hanuman. The throne of Ayodhya is restored to Rama after the period of exile. Subsequently, Ram's subjects ask Sita for proof of her chastity. Sita, who had willingly suffered all hardships, prays for mother earth to accept her if she is indeed pure, and so sacrifices her own life to demonstrate her virtue.

In films, Ram is the conservative son who upholds, or at least does not rebel against, the status quo, which is symbolised by parental authority, the village *panchayat* (council) or the state. He is the son who never shirks his duty, as portrayed by Jackie Shroff in *Ram Lakhan* (Ram & Lakhan, 1989). And the stepson in *Do Raaste* (Two Roads, 1969), played by Balraj Sahni, is not tempted by personal gain. Preferring the family fold, he struggles to keep it intact in the face of divisive forces.

Sita ably supports Ram as he strives to uphold high moral values. Sita's devotion to her husband is unquestioning, and she bears every hardship without complaint. Ram is generally shown as loyal to Sita. In films, such a wife is always demurely clad in traditional attire, helps every member of the joint family and bears the taunts of the mother-in-law or neighbours uncomplainingly. She always waits upon her husband and sticks it out with him through all the vicissitudes of the plot. This type has been cast and recast in many family melodramas over the years. In the 1930s, films like *Gunsundari* (Proper, 1934) probably set the type. The abduction or near-rape of the heroine and her rescue by the hero is a common thematic thread, as in *Tezaab* (Sour, 1988). And in *Khalnayak* (Villain, 1993), after cohabiting with the 'villain' she risks calumny, and must provide proof of her chastity before she can be restored to Ram.

Rama's nobility attracts many devotees and they become his helpers. One is the monkey god Hanuman who is famed and feared for his great strength. In films, however, the antics of the Hanuman-figure provide lighter moments. He may be the hero's friend and ally or his servant, for example the Govinda character to Rajesh Khanna's Rama in *Swarg* (Heaven, 1990). He is either rather nondescript or a comic. He sticks by the hero through thick and thin, although he rarely exhibits the valour or strength of the god he represents. These attributes are reserved exclusively for the hero. He makes impractical suggestions and uses his dull wit to get himself or the hero out of difficult situations. Popular comedians such as Rajendra Nath, Asrani and Johnny Lever have all provided their unique interpretations of this character in films.

ABOVE: **Do Raaste** (1969)
RIGHT: Johnny Lever & Govinda
BELOW: Amitabh Bachchan performing as Hanuman in a song from **Aks** (2001)

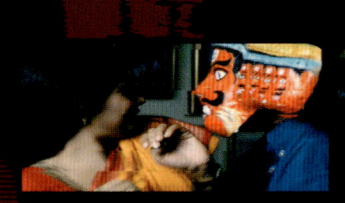 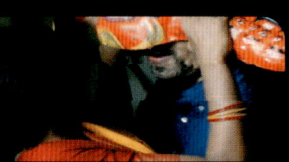  

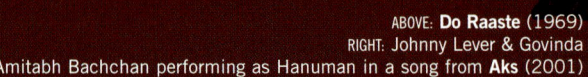

ABOVE: Postcard of Hanuman with the mountain in his hand
BELOW: Ram and Sita

"Go away, Evil" Lord Ram has a bow and arrows

THE MARRIAGE SCENE

BY GAYATRI CHATTERJEE

The primary or secondary narrative thread of more than ninety percent of films produced in India concerns heterosexual love. Couple formation is central to this theme, and in most films the romantic couples ultimately marry. This conclusion represents not only the fruition of romantic love, but also the solution to the social issues each film associates with the love theme: the difference between rich and poor, the caste system and other forms of inequality, the re-establishment of justice, eradication of crime, or any other of a host of other concerns. In many early films social reform and love and marriage were integral to the themes of the films of the time. For example, in *Doctor* (1940) the protagonist combines his idealism with the practice of medicine. Severing ties with his father, and thereby disinherited, he marries a poor, lower caste, girl. For the happy couple, marital love is intrinsically bound up with their services to the village poor.

Kal Ho Na Ho (2003)

Love & Marriage

From a foundation of love and marriage, individuals clash with parental, societal or traditional norms. Marriage ceremonies are dramatically interrupted in several films, in order that men and women eventually wed their true partner – the one they desire and are entitled to be with. In *Chori Chori* (Secretly, 1956), based on *It Happened One Night* (1934), and its most recent remake, *Dil Hai Ki Manta Nahin* (The Heart never listens, 1991), the bride's father urges her to flee her wedding and join the man who truly loves and deserves her. Since the 1943 blockbuster *Kismet* (Destiny), the final frames of many films show the just-married hero or heroine, sometimes driving off in a car, Hollywood style. Occasionally, friends of the hero or heroine also marry, in a double-wedding scene. Other films, which might open with the wedding, portray marital love, marital problems, or both. *Anuradha* (The Love of Anuradha, 1960) and *Anubhav* (Consciousness, 1971) are examples of this genre in which psychological aspects of love and marriage – incompatibility, misunderstanding or miscommunication between the partners – are examined.

Indian films are often preoccupied with the girl's struggle to win the heart of the man she has chosen, and to keep it once he has given it to her. Alternatively, the stories concentrate on her efforts to make members of her husband's family accept and love her since it is not enough that only he should love her.

ABOVE: **Kunku/Duniya Na Maane** (1937)

Social norms are seen to be perpetuated through marriage, and many films show a young bride harassed or physically and mentally tortured by her in-laws. Film-makers are often focused on box office success, and are unsure of how regressive or progressive they should be. Many films, for example *Biwi Ho To Aisi* (The Perfect Wife, 1988), thus become caricatures, and end with all family members reconciled and happy. The relationships between the 'hen-pecked' husband and the 'shrewish' wife, or the submissive wife and the abusive philandering husband, are also popular motifs, but these are usually secondary to the main love interest.

In *Kunku/Duniya Na Maane*[1] (The Unexpected, 1937) a girl is duped into marrying a man old enough to be her father, and she refuses to consummate the marriage. Realising his mistake and wanting to set her free, her husband commits suicide. Problems caused by marriages between young girls and older men are recurring motifs in films of all regions and in all languages, but their treatment and resolution varies.

Some films belonging to the *Muslim social* [2] genre present the Islamic marriage as consensual, with the possibility of the bride refusing to say 'I agree' – as in *Bazaar* (1982).

ABOVE: **Bazaar** (1982)

[1] Marathi and Hindi titles respectively.
[2] Film genre characterised by personal dramas in romanticised Muslim settings.

85

Hum Aapke Hain Kaun (1994)
The 'Shoe Song', one of the many songs in what became the standard for all subsequent 'marriage' films. The film shows the rich tradition of a 'Hindu' marriage with many games and songs as a prologue to the final ceremony.

Kabhi Khushi Kabhie Gam (2003) A 'Muslim' wedding celebration.

Marriages in Hindi films involve large crowds and spectacular shots. Lavish song-and-dance numbers with plenty of colours, food and happiness make a great impression on the viewer.

The wedding scene

Wedding scenes have always been important to Indian films and almost all feature newlyweds in supporting roles. Sooraj Barjatiya's *Hum Aapke Hain Kaun?* (Who Am I To You?, 1994) concerns a successful marriage arranged by two sets of parents. A year later, the bride meets with an accident in late pregnancy, delivers a daughter, and dies. The bride's younger sister has meanwhile fallen in love with the groom's younger brother, but is asked to marry her brother-in-law and raise her niece. The film ends happily when, through the intervention of a domestic servant and a dog, the families come to recognise the younger siblings' love for each other. Journalists and box-office analysts described this phenomenally popular film as a 'wedding-video', referring to the growing trend in India, since the advent of digital cameras, of having home-movies made at weddings by professionals or family members.[3]

Barjatiya's debut film, *Maine Pyaar Kiya* (I Fell In Love, 1989), also a box-office smash, revolved around the romantic love between two young people, and their struggle against parental opposition. The two films illustrate a growing shift in attitude: a greater emphasis on the role of the family rather than the recognition of male-female love as an intimate relationship between two individuals.

Hum Aapke Hain Kaun was followed by several big-budget films featuring elaborate weddings scenes. These films affirmed contemporary urban India's desire to compete in the global marketplace and raise its international profile. Wedding scenes containing unseemly displays of wealth became reminders of 'Indian-ness' to expatriate Indians. They also appealed to members of the Indian urban middle class, who were becoming increasingly alienated from their own environment as a result of their struggle with the effects of increasing consumerism and globalisation. This phenomenon is explored in films such as *Dilwale Dulhaniya Le Jayenge* (The Brave Heart Takes Away the Bride, 1995) and *Kabhi Khushi Kabhie Gham* (Sometimes Happiness Sometimes Sorrow, 2001).[4] Not only mainstream film-makers make films about weddings; artistic directors such as Mira Nair do so too. Although it was produced with international finance and incorporated progressive sub-themes, her *Monsoon Wedding* (*2001*) still addresses the subject of the presentation of traditional weddings while playing upon the Indian joint family structure.

ABOVE: Hema Malini in **Lal Patthar** (1971)

[3] Barjatiya's third film, *Hum Saath Saath Hain* (2001), concerns three brothers who get married and join their father in the family business. As if in response to journalists' and scholars' criticisms that wedding scenes are exclusively Hindu in content, Barjatiya included a Muslim female family-friend shooting videos of the weddings.
[4] Surprisingly, and disturbingly, these films also attempt to create pacts between globalisation and past feudal life in order to re-install virulent patriarchy and rob women of all powers of self-determination.

Khuddaar (1982)

The third angle

The triangular relationship – involving a choice between two lovers or the re-appearance of a former lover after marriage – is a perennially popular theme. In *Gumrah* (Lost, 1963), the woman who must choose between the two men is caught in a moral, not emotional, dilemma. She invariably sacrifices her love interest and faithfully remains with her husband. She learns that what one gets is always 'for the best', as in *Hum Dil De Chuke Sanam* (I've Already Given My Heart, 2000). Another popular dramatic device is the woman who causes a rift in the friendship between two males. In *Sangam* (Confluence, 1964) for example, the characters Sunder and Gopal both love Radha, and she loves Gopal. Ultimately, Gopal makes a sacrifice so that Sunder can marry her, although Radha protests that her wishes are not being considered. After marriage, however, Sunder becomes obsessed by jealousy and fear of her infidelity. Unable to see his friend suffering so much, Gopal tries to prove Radha's innocence and then commits suicide. The introduction of the third player, man or woman, presages a schism between duty and desire – between 'that which is desirable and pleasant to the individual' (*preya*) and 'that which bears the ultimate good and is beneficial to all' (*shreya*). This discourse, borrowed from Vedic and Upanishadic texts, was important to nationalist thinkers in the early period of nationalism.

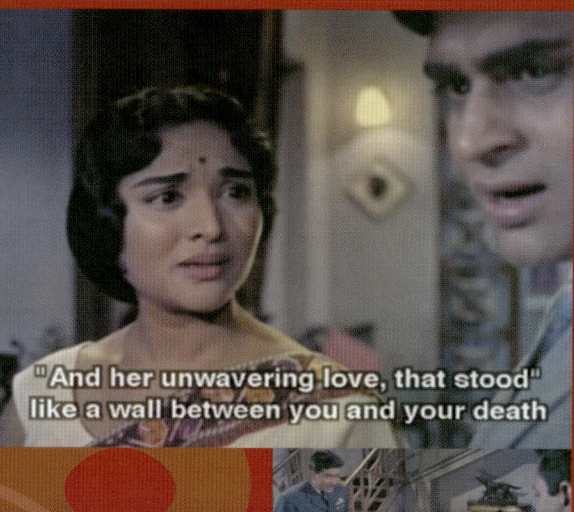

ABOVE: **Hum Dil De Chuke Sanam** (2000)
LEFT: **Sangam** (1964)
BELOW: **Kal Ho Naa Ho** (2003)

Ritual marks

The *bindi* is a red dot of vermilion powder worn between the eyebrows or on the forehead by girls and women. It is a symbol of Goddess Parvati and signifies female energy. It is believed to protect women and their husbands. Traditionally a symbol of marriage, nowadays it is used as decoration and is worn today by unmarried girls and women as well. No longer restricted in colour or shape, *bindis* are seen in various designs and bright colours. They may also be made of felt and embellished with glass or glitter.

The *mangalsutra* is a necklace of two strings of black beads with a gold pendant. It is worn only by women as a sign of being married; the Indian equivalent of the Western wedding ring. The groom ties the *mangalsutra* around his bride's neck.

The *tilak* is a ritual mark on the forehead. It is a sign of blessing or greeting. It is usually made of a red vermilion paste (*kumkum*) that is a mixture of tumeric, alum, camphor and iodine. It can also be made of sandalwood paste (*chandan*) blended with musk. The *tilak* is applied between the eyebrows, which is considered the seat of latent wisdom and mental concentration. It indicates the location where the spiritual eye opens. All Hindu rites and ceremonies begin by placing a *tilak* with the tip of the index finger or thumb. The same custom is followed when welcoming or bidding farewell to guests or relations.

ABOVE: **Mother India** (1957)

Marriage signs

The signs of marriage eternally mark the female body: the vermilion that reddens a woman's hair parting over her forehead, the *bindi* (red dot) on her forehead between her eyebrows, or the black and gold beaded necklace around her neck.[5]

The woman is objectified in mainstream cinema: the female figure in film represents traditional social values – female docility, respectfulness and obedience – and this symbolism must never to be disturbed. Moreover, it falls to the female figure herself to guard and perpetuate this role at all costs. Discussions of tradition and change may continue, but she is the ultimate symbol of that tradition and is expected to be unchanging.

In *Sahib Bibi aur Ghulam* (Master, Mistress and Servant, 1962), a wife belonging to a feudal joint family secretly buys a brand of red vermilion she believes will miraculously preserve marital bliss. But the patriarchs of the family wrongly suspect her because of her secrecy and the extreme measures she adopts in order to win her husband's love; and they kill her.

Divine couples and medieval love stories

Written and oral Indian myths and medieval love stories are prototypes for many films about love. Broadly speaking, there are three types of archetypical love stories in India: the marital love between Shiva and Parvati, and Rama and Sita; the extra-marital love between Krishna and Radha and other *gopis*, (cow-herding girls); and the doomed love between young men and women – princes and princesses. The first two come from Hindu mythology and the third from the Sufi Islamic tradition of telling secular love stories to invoke spirituality.

In all her incarnations as Sati and Uma, Parvati goes against the wishes of her father, and prays extensively and carries out acts of penance to get the ascetic and maverick god Shiva as her husband. Once married, Shiva falls madly in love with her; they live in intense marital bliss and have a son, the elephant-headed Ganesh. Representations of wives taking care of husbands in simple ways and without regard to personal welfare, evoke folk stories about this divine couple.

One of India's greatest and most popular epics, the Ramayana, centres on the monogamous marriage between Ram and Sita that ends in war and separation. Because of her desire for a golden deer, a series of disasters befalls Sita, including abduction and trial by fire; her return is followed by an idyllic fourteen-year-long exile together with Ram in a forest. Ram has to make her endure these trials in compliance with the wishes of his people, and she ultimately leaves him to return to Mother Earth. Thereafter, Ram grieves for her and leads the life of a tragic hero.

The Radha-Krishna legend is more difficult to describe due to its complexity. The love between them, illicit and powerfully spiritual, has marked Indian cinema more than any other (see 'Lost in Love', page 76).

Almost as important are the traditional Arabic love stories from medieval Persia that circulated in India and produced new bodies of literature in local languages. *Love & God* (1986) is based on one such story concerning the legendary Laila and Majnu. Film titles sometimes celebrate the names of the couple and there are, for example, over half a dozen films with the title *Heer Ranjha*. These films are not only about extreme passion in love, but also the impossibility of obtaining the object of one's love. And thus they deal with the close relation between love and death.

Death might be a desirable end to a life without love, but the idea that lovers are destined for each other is more pleasant – that they are connected not just in this life but over several reincarnations, as in *Madhumati* (1958). Love is a given in Indian films, for love is destiny. Men and women wish to be married to the same partners over several lives. Love never dies; it is perpetuated over aeons and many lifetimes and is, as it were, 'frozen' in marriage.

[5] There are vast regional variations: at times determined by clan or cast rules, at times by geography. But today, sadly, wedding scenes are becoming increasingly standardised.

"The world of my dreams lies shattered"

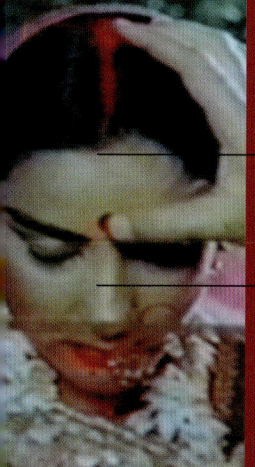

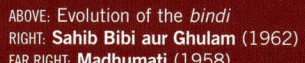
ABOVE: Evolution of the *bindi*
RIGHT: **Sahib Bibi aur Ghulam** (1962)
FAR RIGHT: **Madhumati** (1958)

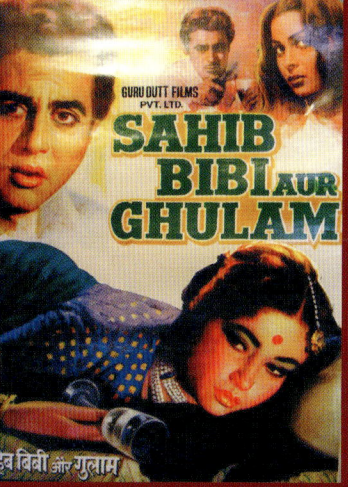

"I have lost the love I once had"

THE ENEMY

BY: FAREEDA

TOP/FAR RIGHT: Promotional mask book **Lagaan**
ABOVE/RIGHT: **Lagaan** (2001)

Ever since the arrival of cinema in India, film-makers have searched for a way to define the Indian national identity in relation to its enemies. No single image has endured. The nature of cinema has evolved along with the nature of the state. The concepts of 'us' and 'the enemy' have been constantly redefined in the Indian film industry, as they have been in Hollywood.

Anti-colonial nationalist films attempted to unite the people and preserve an essential purity, for example by recalling a golden age later poisoned by 'outsiders' – variously referred to as *videshi*, *angerz* or *gore* (foreigners, English, or white skinned).

Phalke's *Kaliya Mardan* (Slaying of the Snake, 1919) can be interpreted as one such nationalist allegory in which the seemingly powerless manage to overcome their oppressor. Complete with special effects, it shows the child Krishna slaying the snake demon *Kaliya Mardan* who poisons the waters of the river Yamuna and wreaks havoc on the population. We return to this theme in *Lagaan* (Land Tax, 2001), which revolves around the greed and cruelty of the British and the response of some villagers challenged to a very unfair cricket match.

LEFT: Gandhi facing criticism in **The Legend of Bhagat Singh** (2002)

94

LEFT: Advertisement for **Do Bigha Zamin** (1953)
ABOVE: Moneylender in **Mother India** (1957)

Later, after the representatives of the Crown had gone, their culture was lampooned to attenuate any remaining influence it had. This hostility to Western mores and values was most obvious in the work of actor, director and producer Manoj Kumar. *Purav aur Paschim* (East and West, 1975), for example, concerns a cigarette-smoking girl who returns and becomes 'Indianised'.

Post independence, the nation had a progressive agenda and there was an urge to modernise.[1] The old feudal order and its social structures were seen as impeding planned economic changes. Enemies were thus portrayed as forces existing within decadent feudalistic structures – caste prejudice, the moneylender, the landlord – in films such as *Sujata* (Sujata 1959) and *Mother India* (1957).

ABOVE: **Purav aur Paschim** (1975)
BELOW: **Mr. India** (1987)

In modern films, this 'enemy within' has taken the form of corrupt politicians, businessmen, police and unscrupulous professionals who ransack national wealth for private profit. *Mr. India* (1987), *Krantiveer* (Hero of the Revolution, 1994) and *Hindustani* (The Indian, 1996) are films in this vein; they are often orgies of violence involving the spectator in sado-masochistic fantasies of retribution.

Geopolitically, India's enemies were Pakistan and China, but the war film is not a very popular genre in Indian cinema. *Haqeeqat* (Truth, 1964), which focuses on Sino-Indian tensions, is an exception. Pakistan is the implied enemy in the plot of many films, however, including *Lakshya* (The Objective, 2004) and *Deewaar* (The Wall, 2004).

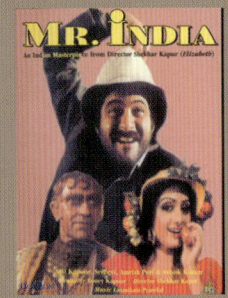

In the hands of film-makers, separatist movements become tools for generating sentiment for an undivided India. The political scenario is sometimes used as a thrilling backdrop to a more personal tale of a well-knit family, or of a loving couple torn asunder by misdirected militants, as in *Roja* (Rose, 1992).

[1] As Madhav Prasad elucidates in his book *Ideology of the Hindi Film, A Historical Construction*, Oxford University Press, 1998.

Wall poster and postcard of *Gadar*

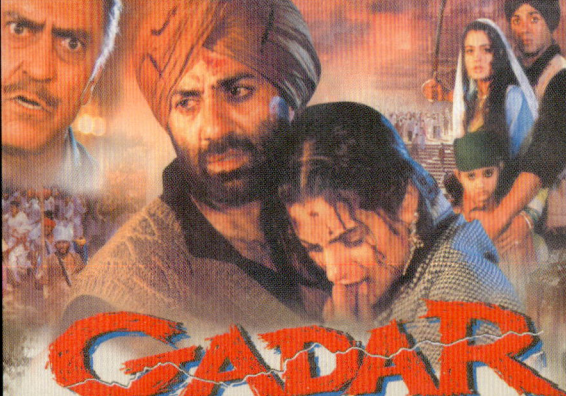

Haqeeqat (1964)

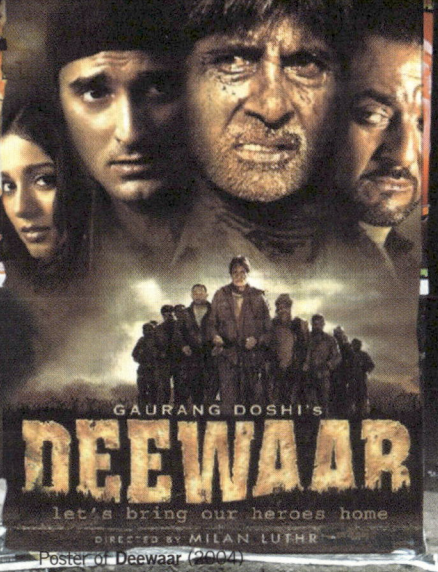

LEFT & BELOW: **Roja** (1992)

Poster of Deewaar (2004)

97

Following India's partition into Muslim Pakistan and Hindu India, it is assumed that politically conscious Hindus are nationalists with no conflicting loyalties. Indian Muslims, however, are often suspected by compatriots of primary allegiance to their Islamic brethren and to Pakistan; pressure continues to be exerted on them to prove their commitment to the Indian nation. This theme is explored in *Sarfarosh* (They Who Sacrifice, 1999). Although mainstream cinema does not overtly portray such community themes, non-Hindus are very often exoticised or caricatured.

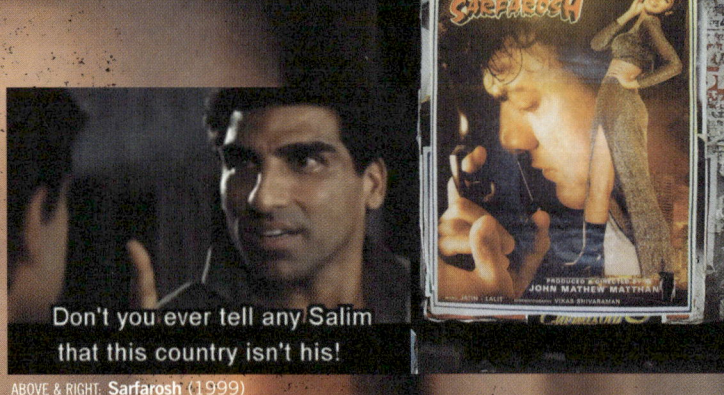

ABOVE & RIGHT: **Sarfarosh** (1999)
BELOW: Cassette, DVD and scenes from **Dil Se** (1998), a film about the separatist movement in North East India.

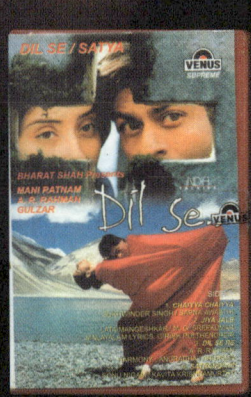
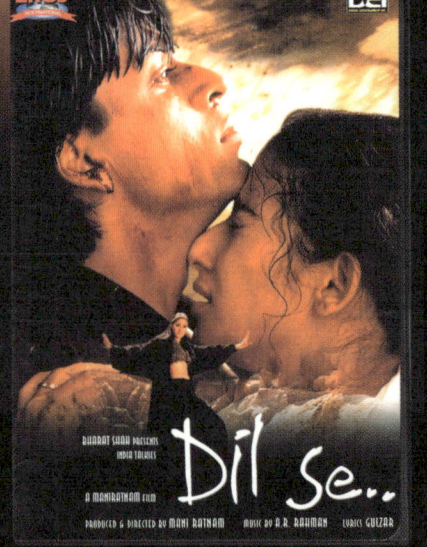

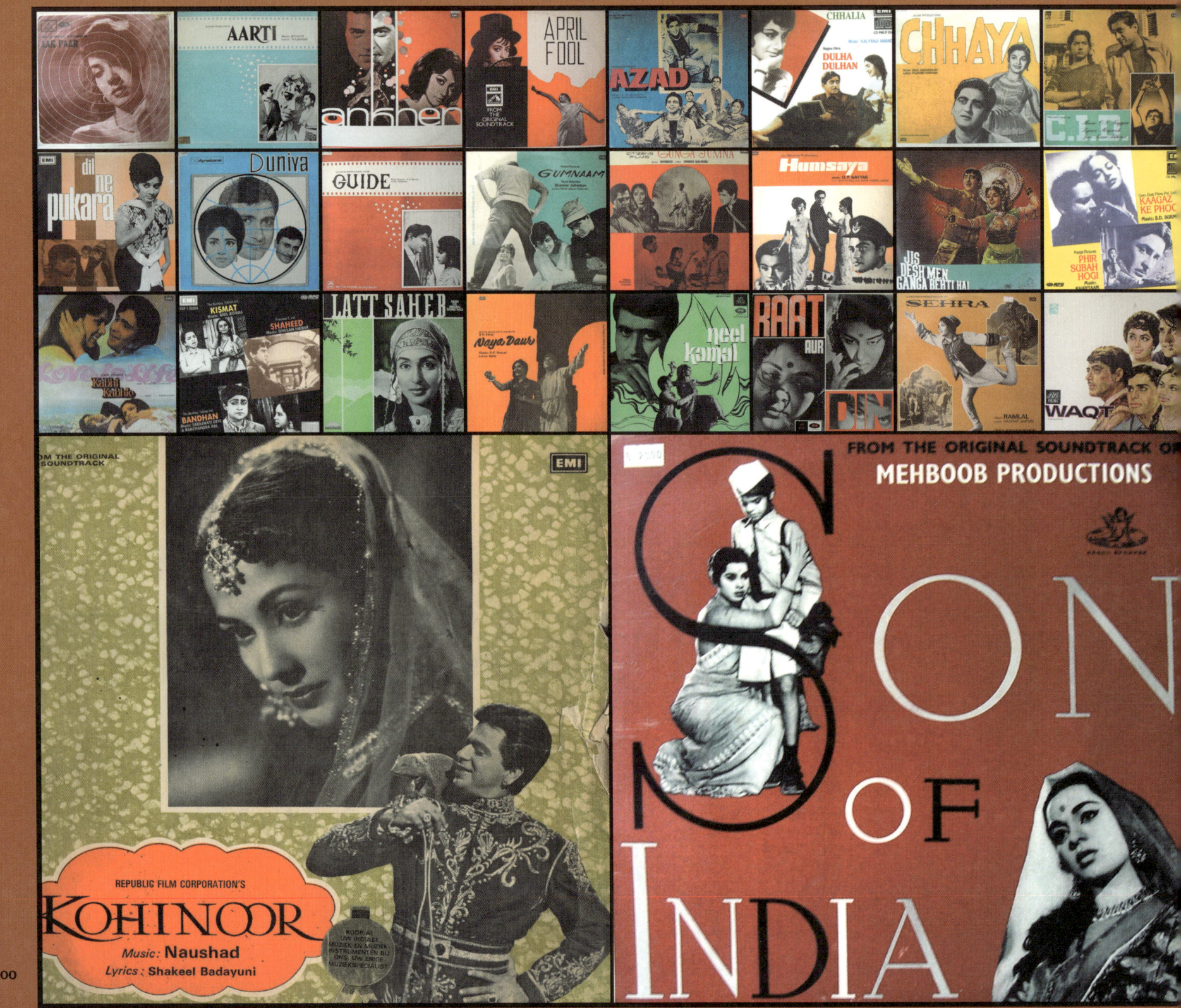

SONGS

BY: BRAHMANAND SINGH

LEFT PAGE: **Kohinoor** (1960), **Son of India** (1962)
ABOVE: Audio cassettes

Walk anywhere in India — marketplaces, festive centres or domestic parties, villages, towns or cities — and it is almost impossible that popular film songs will not be inundating your ears. With their melodious quality and excellent poetry, film songs have made many films part of the nation's collective psyche over the years.

In India, film music is big business, worth billions of rupees. The producer can recover a substantial part of his overall production investment with the sale of music rights alone.

With the first Indian talkie, *Alam Ara* (The Light of the World, 1931) by Ardeshir Irani, songs came to be regarded as indispensable elements in Indian films. Between 1931 and 1940 India produced over nine hundred Hindi feature films with an average of ten songs per film. The numbers of songs in regional films from Chennai and Kolkata were much lower, but the importance of music was similar. Trends in Hindi film songs have invariably influenced regional cinema in Tamil, Telugu and Bengali, rather than the other way round.

With his unique voice and style, Kundelal Lal Saigal sang his way into the hearts of the Indian masses, who became delirious on hearing songs from *Devdas* (Devdas, 1935), *Kapaal Kundala* (Kapaal Kundala, 1939), *Dushman* (The Enemy, 1938) and *Street Singer* (1938). In *Street Singer,* Saigal's rendition of *Babul Mora* was sung live as he 'walked the streets' in the studio, with the entire orchestra following him just off screen. The result was magical.

The song dealt with separation. It was composed by the legendary Nawab Wajid Ali Shah of Lucknow in the nineteenth century, when he was banished from his beloved hometown by the East India Company. Overnight, *Babul Mora* became the country's most poignant farewell song. K.L. Saigal's simple but soulful rendition of this *Bhairavi Thumri*[1] made people cry and is a popular song at most marriage farewells to this day.[2]

O my father, I'm bidding goodbye to my home
Four men and a resplendent palanquin I get
But those I call my own, I have to leave.

My own piazza is no longer mine,
My own gates are now a foreign land,
O my father, I hand over my home to you,
As I leave for my husband's abode.[3]

The mass appeal of the songs notwithstanding, good sound-recording facilities were not yet available and composers had to resort to numerous innovative techniques. A minimum of instruments were used because the musicians had to be camouflaged behind the singer/actor, and everything had to be done with the camera rolling.

And so the story goes that during the filming of a song in the late 1930s, an actress became agitated while singing a song because the *tabla*[4] beat was going haywire. When they stopped to check what the matter was, the tabla player explained that a fish had entered inside his loincloth! The hapless musician was hidden in a pool below the actress, so that her microphone could record his part without him being seen.

Although actors sang their own songs for most of the decade, towards the late 1930s the system of playback singing was introduced by the director Nitin Bose. Thus began the era of singers; their voices were used for popular actors such as Ashok Kumar, Leela Chitnis, Devika Rani and Moti Lal, most of whom were not comfortable singing.

[1] A light Indian classical music genre, usually sung as the finale of a vocal classical concert.
[2] A bride must often leave her blood-family to live far away with her husband's relatives.
[3] The original Hindi text of all songs mentioned, and information about the film in which they featured, can be found at the end of this chapter.
[4] Percussion instrument that provides rhythmic structure to songs, instrumental music and dances.

LEFT: Still from **Street Singer** (1938)
ABOVE: K.L. Saigal

music. NAUSHAD

MUSIC: C. RAMCHANDRA
LYRICS: RAJINDER KRISHAN

Music: Rajesh Roshan
Lyrics: Anand Bakshi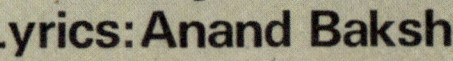

three faces of Man
music khayyam lyrics sahir

MUSIC SHANKER JAIKISHAN

 MUSIC LAXMIKANT PYARELAL

MUSIC: GHULAM MOHAMMED

Music: GHULAM HAIDER 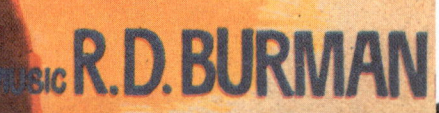 Music R.D. BURMAN  MUSIC KALYANJI ANANDJI

The Blossoming of Indian film music

Film songs as a genre started to blossom in the 1940s. Great singers, including Noorjahan, Shamshad Begum, Zohra Bai and K.L. Saigal, were later joined by the likes of Lata Mangeshkar, Mohammad Rafi, Manna Dey, Mukesh and Suraiya, and with their contributions film songs developed into a genuine art form.

Composers such as Kemchand Prakash, Anil Biswas, Naushad and Shankar Jaikishen, in collaboration with lyricists Behzad Lucknavi, Hasrat Jaipuri, Shakeel Badyuni, Majrooh Sultanpuri and others, churned out one hit after another.

In spite of a large number of hits, technically these were still the primitive days, and inventiveness was called for. Songs were recorded on a single channel; very often outdoors in a garden or open place. Recordings were invariably made after midnight in order to minimise extraneous noise. On cue, a flute player would have to tiptoe to the single microphone and play his part. His distance from the singer had to be just right to avoid sounding too loud. He then had to tiptoe away again, so that the other instrumentalist could take his position.

Just to create the effect of an echo, for example, the composer Naushad had to record four prints of the same sound, with the volume control at 100, 70, 30 and 10 percent respectively, and then mix them judiciously on the opticals themselves to get the desired effect on a single track.

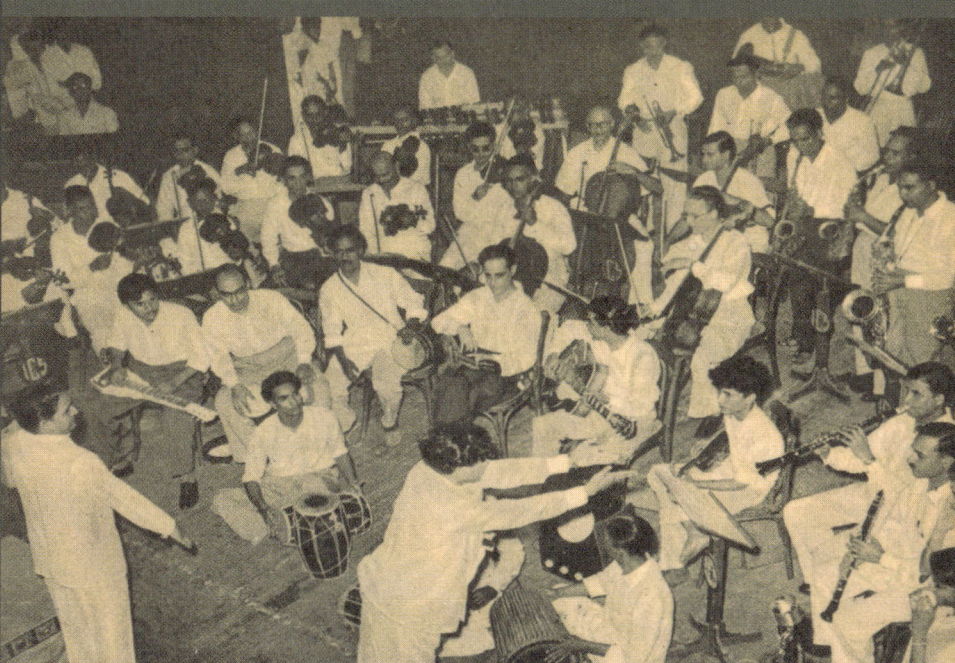

ABOVE: Shanker (left) and Jaikishen
Right: Shanker and Jaikishen working with their musicans, who play both Western and Indian instruments.
(*Filmfare*, 6 February 1953)

The best harvest of Hindi film songs

The 1950s were undisputedly the golden years of Indian film music. Never before in the history of music had we been able to hear such tantalising lyrics and euphonious compositions.

Lata Mangeshkar, Mohammad Rafi, Mukesh, Talat Mehmood, Geeta Dutt, Asha Bhosle, Suraiya and Kishore Kumar and other illustrious artistes were established playback singers.

The blockbusters *Mahal* (The Palace, 1949), *Barsaat* (Rain, 1948), *Awaara* (The Vagabond, 1951), *Shree 420* (Mr. 420, 1955), *Nagin* (The Snake, 1954), *Bazaar* (1949), *Andaz* (Nuance, 1948), *Naya Daur* (New Era, 1957), *Soneki Chidiya* (Golden Cage, 1958), *Howrah Bridge* (1958), *Phagun* (Month of Spring, 1958), *Pyaasa* (Eternal Thirst, 1957) *Kaagaz Ke Phool* (Paper Flowers, 1959), *Mother India* (1957) and many other films swept the country and left the public gasping for more.

Film companies mushroomed, and some of the most melodious songs of all time were written in this period. Music directors, including S.D. Burman, C. Ramchandra, Madan Mohan, Naushad Ali, O.P. Nayyar, Salil Chowdhury and Roshan, started commanding adulation of the masses in no uncertain terms. At the beginning of the 1950s, the song *Awaara Hoon* (*Awaara*, 1951), written by Shailendra, became a phenomenal success. The film, and particularly the title song, swept through Asia. And even if borrowed from Chaplin, Raj Kapoor's trademark image – rolled-up trousers, patched jacket and bowler hat – struck a chord with audiences both at home and abroad.

I am a vagabond
Or perhaps, a star in the firmament
I don't have a home, I don't have ties
No one to love me, no one to wait for
Lonely roads and unfamiliar cities are my only friends
Unloved, uncelebrated
I still sing happy songs
Maybe tormented inside
Still, I always sport smiling eyes
Pierced by the arrows of the world or perhaps of destiny
I am a vagabond
Or perhaps, a star in the firmament

Sung by Mukesh, the tramp song was a mixture of melodrama, romance and lightness of being. It became an allegory for the innocent state of mind of the post-independence Indian who identified with Raj Kapoor's rootless vagabond (*awaara*) when the entire socio-political system was under stress and thousands of migrants were pouring into the cities.

People of a reflective nature were charmed by the integral beauty and lyricism of songs like *Waqt Ne Kiya Kya Hasin Sitam* (*Kaagaz Ke Phool*, 1959). It was a melancholic contemplation of the changes wrought by time, and became one of the biggest hits of those years.

Time has caught us both in its warp
You are not your own self anymore, nor am I mine
Former lovers, we meet once again
As though we never parted, never felt the pain
Only to lose our steps towards each other once again
Where do we go, can't fathom much
We've stepped out indeed, without knowing for where
Don't even know what we are searching for
Just weaving dreams with every breath

Geeta Dutt's pain-lashed voice and S.D. Burman's soulful tune added a soft devastation to Kaifi Azmi's poetry that moved people deeply. Director Guru Dutt, playing the role of a tormented film-maker, added much to the layers of irony and philosophy of coming to terms with isolation and emptiness. His brooding sensitivity added to this simple song a glow of romanticism that stupefies and disturbs at the same time.

There were other songs that could bowl one over with their unassuming poetry. Sahir Ludhianvi,[5] well known for transferring progressive Urdu literature to Hindi film lyrics, was a poet with remarkable musical sensibility, and he inspired various forms of radical music. Take for example, his lines in a tragic song such as *Jayen to Jayen Kahan* in *Taxi Driver* (1954):

Where do I go?
Who'll decode my language of pain?
I carry a carnival of sorrow inside me,
What else is left for me in life?
Soul trapped in despair, heart caught in sorrow
My pain is compounded by the ones of my beloved
It's difficult now to survive
It's like one boat against hundreds of tempests

LEFT: **Awaara** (1951)

Or in the song *Jaane Wo Kaise Log The Jinke* in *Pyaasa* (1957), especially when he says:

If this is what life is all about, I too will live it out
I won't complain, I'll seal my pain, I'll gulp my own tears
What's there to fear about sorrow when you get it a hundred times?

In *Mother India* (1957), *Duniyan Mein Hum Aayen Hain To*, by composer Naushad, exemplifies a remarkable, almost epic, dauntlessness. It is performed by a rural Indian woman, Radha (played by popular star Nargis), who has fallen on hard times after the loss of her husband. Nargis, in the voice of Lata Mangeshkar, sings:

We have been born, never to give up
If adversity makes us stumble, we will rise up each time we fall
If it means walking on fire, we will not flinch even once

Or a little later in the same song:

It takes a woman of substance to know what's her shame and what's not
She who will live with dignity will remain dignified even in death

She became the ultimate 'Indian Woman', respected by all, as in the song *O Jaane Walo* when she sings her plea to the villagers not to leave their place of origin:

Don't go away from your mother earth
This is your village, your lanes, your fields
So what if a little distraught or a little less fertile
It is your mother who calls you to her.

She actually succeeds in preventing the exodus from the village, and starts off a movement based on dignity and hard work rather than on an easy way out.

There are elements in the film that reach deep into the Indian psyche, and it struck a chord that had never been struck before. With *Mother India*, Mehboob Khan gave Indian cinema its archetypal 'mother' myth. She is both

---

[5] Member of the Progressive Writers' Association (PWA), which was rooted in the anti-imperialist struggle and made up of committed leftist writers. Sadat Hassan Manto, Ismat Chughtai, Mulk Raj Anand, Faiz Ahmed Faiz, Jan Nisar Akhtar, Ali Sardar Jafri, Sahir Ludhianvi, Majrooh Sultanpuri, Kaifi Azmi were among the members. They held considered debates on various issues. Their literary output for films and other media was a powerful tool for reaching out to the masses and communicating the ideal of a future classless society.

[6] It was the first Indian film to be nominated for an Oscar, in 1958

a woman and an equal partner in her husband's labours. The combined effect of several songs in this film makes a huge impact on viewers even today.[6]

In the 1950s, a formula for popular success consisting of song, dance, spectacle and fantasy was established in Indian cinema that continues to be used in modern times. Powerful poetry, soulful music and its impact on audiences helped film become recognised as a significant instrument of social criticism. The directors V. Shantaram, Bimal Roy, Guru Dutt, Mehboob Khan and Raj Kapoor, and others, made considerable impact on art, politics and social life. One of the main reasons for this was that they were able to reach out to the masses through a shared aspect of their cinema: song.

ABOVE: Kaagaz Ke Phool *(1959)*

LEFT: **Mother India** *(1957)*

The teenage years

For popular film songs, the 1960s was a time of relative stability during which popular cinema gradually shifted towards more romantic genres. However, films that focused on social concerns and had good music continued to be made, as they had in the 1950s. New stars appeared, among them Shammi Kapoor, the Indian Elvis, and later Rajesh Khanna, the romantic hero.

In many ways these were the teenage years for Indian film music. Western influences openly filtered into the scene, encouraging a sort of fusion music in such hit films as *Dil Tera Diwana* (My Heart is Crazy about you, 1962), *An Evening in Paris* (1967), *Teesri Manzil* (The Third Floor, 1966), *Jewel Thief* (1967) and *Aradhana* (Aradhana, 1969).

Towards the second half of the decade, another phenomenon arrived on the scene: R.D. Burman. Using drums, bongos, trumpets, flutes, electric guitars, keyboards, frenzied percussion and swinging melodies, he ushered a strongly rock 'n' roll-influenced trend into Hindi film music. It was there to stay. Almost all the songs from his debut film *Teesri Manzil* (The Third Floor, 1966) were phenomenal hits, and one particular cabaret number, *O Haseena Zulfon Wali* (O You Beauty With Lustrous Tresses) sung by Mohammad Rafi and Asha Bhosle, caught the imagination of music lovers across the country.

The song is extremely entertaining; the latent lovers, played by Asha Parekh and Shammi Kapoor, play hide-and-seek with their confessions of their love for each other. Enlivened by Helen's foot-tapping and sensuous dance, which dominates the screen, the catchy melody with its inimitable rhythm and pace had everyone gasping in erotic suspense with lines like:

I'm looking for that stranger
I'm looking for that lover
The one who has hidden himself after lighting the fire inside me,
I'm looking for that moth

Sung in answer to:

O you beauty with lustrous tresses
Whom the killer eyes
Search for its target?

Not only does it make for some witty and wonderfully poetic repartee, but it also builds up the ironic romance, playing on the word *Qatil* (killer) again and again with tease, tension and tenor in this murder mystery. After *Teesri Manzil*, cabaret dances by Helen or other stars including Bindu or Padma Khanna became regular fixtures in countless films,

While R.D. charmed the young with these and other triumphant numbers, his father S.D. Burman and Naushad continued to reign supreme with their soulful and powerful melodies. Maestro Naushad's composition *Pyar Kiya To Darna Kiya* (What's There to Fear About Being in Love?) in K. Asif's magnum opus *Mughal-e-Azam* (The Great Moghul, 1960) was set in a hall of mirrors, reflecting the servant girl Anarkali in an endless kaleidoscopic effect. She confronts the court with the truth while singing in front of the Emperor Akbar, whose wrath she has incurred because she is a commoner in love with his son Salim.

To live with love, to die with love
When we don't have to hide anything from my God,
Why do we have to care for men around me?

The song represents a unique, defiant and youthful love that is in conflict with, and thwarted by, convention and authority. It provides rich dramatic material for the epic love story and has immense popular appeal.
Produced at a cost of fifteen million rupees (about US $300,000), it was the costliest Indian film of its time. The song, shot in the specially-built Sheesh Mahal (Glass Palace) and sung by Lata Mangeshkar, is a tribute to the imagination, hard work and lavishness of its maker. Simultaneously erotic, sensuous and sensitive, this impassioned dance performance by actress Madhubala as Anarkali is unmatched in its grandeur and beauty to this day.

BELOW & RIGHT: **Mughal-e-Azam** (1960)

The remarkable thing about the music of the 1960s was that so many people were able to produce numbers that were sheer gems in artistry and appeal. Take, for example *Abhi Na Jao Chodkar*, Jaidev's soulful and sensuous music to Sahir Ludhianvi's lines in *Hum Dono* (The Two of Us, 1961), in which the lovers express their need, hesitance and vulnerability to each other with witty eroticism:

You have just arrived;
Your presence is still in its spring
Let the breeze embrace your fragrance,
Let my eyes feast a little
Let the evening go down a little,
Let my heart recover a little
We haven't yet said a word,
We haven't heard a thing.

Or take Ravi's title track from *Chaudhvin Ka Chand* (The Fourteenth Day of the Moon, 1960) with Shakeel Badayuni's poetry:

Tresses like clouds hanging on your shoulder
Eyes like sparkling wine brimming the cup
You are a wine whose inebriation is love
Face, like a blooming lotus in the lake
Or like a song played on life's harp
Sweetheart, you are a poet's dream composition

In the 1960s, playback singers started becoming strongly associated with the onscreen stars. By matching their demeanour and vocal style, and singing for them, playback singers created the illusion that the actors were themselves singing. Mohammad Rafi as the voice of Dilip Kumar, Rajendra Kumar and Shammi Kapoor; Mukesh as that of Raj Kapoor and Manoj Kumar; and Kishore Kumar as Dev Anand's and Rajesh Khanna's voices, gained widespread acceptance. In a similar way, Lata Mangeshkar represented the voice of most of the leading lady stars, while her sister Asha Bhosle's voice was invariably associated with the vamps and courtesans.

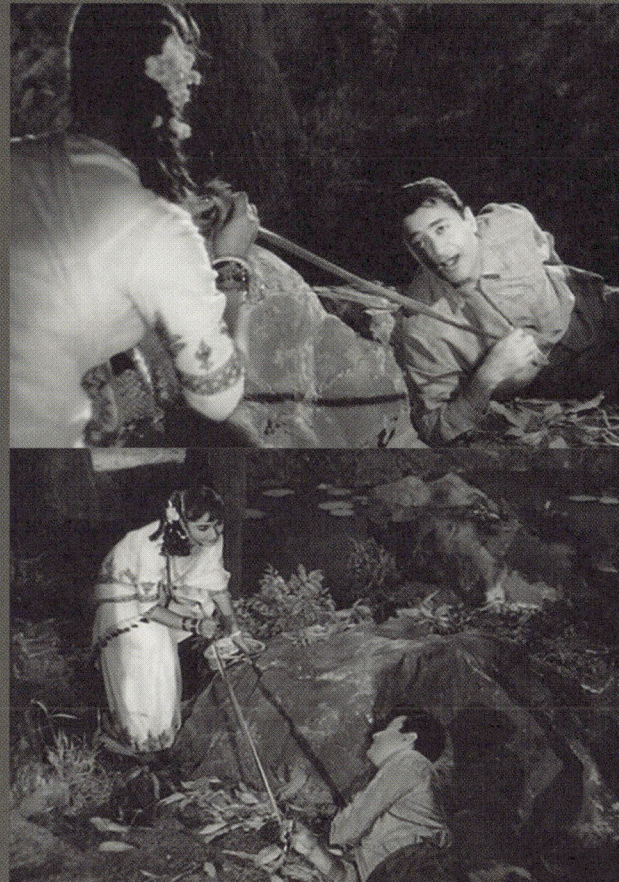

ABOVE: **Hum Dono** (1961)

ABOVE & RIGHT: **Chaudhvin Ka Chand** (1960)

Shifting trends

The release of *Aradhana* (1969) gave India its first superstar: Rajesh Khanna. In the 1970s, Khanna had some of the greatest and most memorable hits of his career through singer and actor Kishore Kumar, who also sang some of the finest poetic songs of the decade for Dev Anand's screen personae. The song *Phoolon Ke Rang Se* from *Prem Pujari* (The Devotee of Love, 1970) is one such example:

When I closed my eyes, I dreamt of you alone
When I remained awake, I thought of nothing but you
I remained enwrapped in your thoughts like flower and string
Our love is like the cloud and its lightning
Like the sandalwood and its wetness
So very tender and just a little tenuous and intoxicated
Our love stands the test of endless rebirths

However, the really big hits of the decade were songs like *Dum Maro Dum* (Let's Get Stoned on Pot) from *Hare Rama Hare Krishna* (1971):

What have we received from the world?
What has the world given us ever?
Why should we be bothered about anyone?
Whatever has anyone ever done for us?

Songs such as these ushered in an age of commercial and even vulgar artificiality, in which romance, innocence and eroticism were sidelined, and violence took an increasingly prominent role. Audience taste had also changed. By and large, films had lost much of their earlier lyricism and charm.

ABOVE: Rajesh Khanna

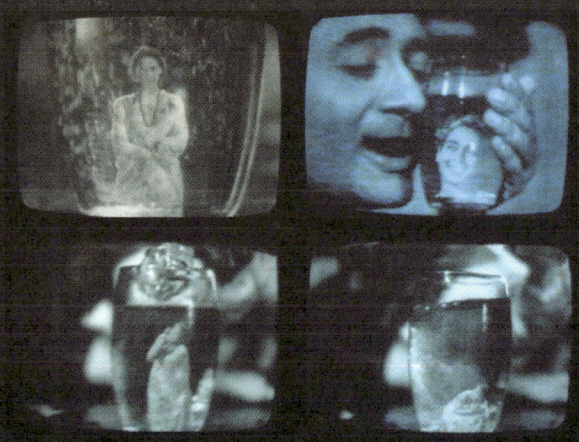

ABOVE: Dev Anand and Nutan in **Tere Ghar Ke Saamne** (1963)

The loss of lyricism

Musically, the 1980s started with a bang. First there were soppy love stories, for example *Ek Duje Ke Liye* (For Each Other, 1980) and *Love Story* (1980). These were soon followed by *Umrao Jaan* (*Umrao Jaan*, 1981), a period classic. The story concerned a nineteenth century courtesan who was a respected musician and dancer. The film temporarily revived the sixties music of love and romance. Umrao Jaan's songs, composed by Khayyam and written by Shahryar, are sheer poetry, and the film had some memorable *ghazals* (lyric poetry, often set to music) like *Dil Cheez Kya Hai* (What Kind of Thing is the Heart?) and *In Aankhon Ki Masti* (My Intoxicating Eyes). They were wonderfully evocative of the poetry-smitten world of nineteenth-century Islamic urban culture, in which all educated people were aspiring Urdu poets. Viewed through the prism of Umrao Jaan's intensely personal experiences – sensual, delicately filigreed – the song *In Aankhon Ki Masti* paints images of the pathos and alienation of a courtesan without ever compromising the tremulous intensity of the power she exerts over her admirers.

My intoxicating eyes have a thousand admirers
My intoxicating eyes will tell you a thousand tales
You're not the only one
Whose love I have not returned
The city hides a thousand such paramours of mine
A lamp like me fears no storm
There are a thousand moths
Who'll form my shield

The opulent *mise en scène* of Umrao's exquisite locations; the shimmering costumes of dazzling brocade and gauzy muslin; the plaintive notes of the *sarangi*;[7] the carpets, hookahs, silver, *paan*,[8] boxes, crystal lamps, and the Vermeer-like mirrors that confront Umrao with her own melancholy at every turn in her eventful journey; and not least, the hypnotic impact of actress Rekha's lustrous eyes: all this is nothing less than devastating.

---

[7] An instrument resembling the violin, with horse-gut strings. It is renowned for its plaintive sound.
[8] *Paan* consists of a betel leaf wrapped around a mixture of lime paste, spices, areca nut and often tobacco – which makes it addictive. This preparation is chewed. It is associated with luxury and decadence.

ABOVE & LEFT: **Umrao Jaan** (1981)

My intoxicating eyes have a thousand admirers
My intoxicating eyes will tell you a thousand tales
You're not the only one
Whose love I have not returned

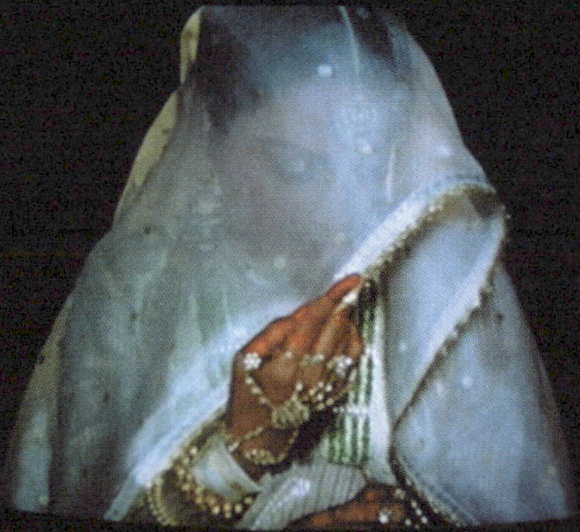

The city hides a thousand such paramours of mine
There are a thousand moths
A lamp like me fears no storm
Who'll form my shield

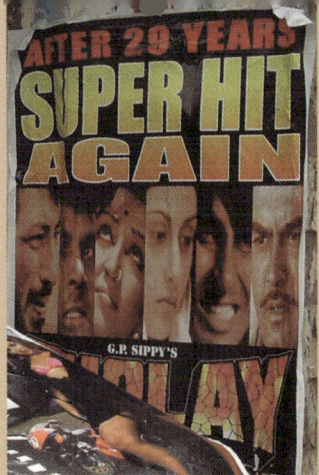

LEFT: **Zanjeer** (1973)
RIGHT: **Sholay** (1975), re-released in 2004
BELOW: **Trishul** (1978), poster, dialogue record, soundtrack LP and bonus 7 inch

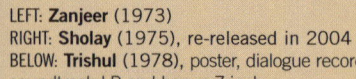

However, apart from a few exceptions such as these, the quality of film music declined drastically and lyrics were generally unremarkable. Films became violent and titillating, rather than romantic and sensuous. What the audience got to see were the 'angry young man' films starring Amitabh Bachchan looming larger than life.

Before Bachchan, movies had more dramatic irony in their narrative and were generally more romantic. With *Namak Haram* (Disloyal) and *Zanjeer* (Chains) in 1973, Amitabh introduced an unrefined realism into mainstream Indian cinema, a genre that gave rise to a series of ill-planned, plotless movies, with largely gratuitous action.

Interestingly, following the release of *Sholay* (Flames, 1975), a mega-film by any standard, LPs and cassettes of its soundtrack sold for the first time in Indian film history for the hard-hitting dialogue rather than the songs.

Heroines such as Zeenat Aman and Parveen Babi introduced a form of on-screen sexuality that was associated only with the cabaret dancers and vamps of the past. And the trendy disco style, with pelvic thrusts and lewd gyrating movements, became more popular by the day.

LEFT: **Deewaar** (1975), dialogue record

Mixed fare, mostly disappointing

With the influx of cable television in the 1990s it became difficult to categorise audience taste. Violence and sex, a legacy of the earlier Bachchan era, seemed to be the safest bet. Then along came *Choli Ke Peechhe Kya Hai* (*Khalnayak*, The Villain, 1993), which become a rage and set a trend for dirty ditties:

What's there under your blouse
Under my blouse, is my heart
Which I'll be giving only to my lover

Crass lyrics based on sexuality and double entendre brought unimaginative songs to an all-time low. What director Subhash Ghai had created as a one-off with *Choli Ke Peechhe Kya Hai* became a regular feature.

One man stood tall amidst the ruins of Hindi film music, otherwise populated by a generation of mediocre composers: A.R. Rahman from Chennai. He grew up on a staple diet of Tamil film songs and served a short apprenticeship with Tamil composer Ilaiyaraja, one of the most respected figures in the field. In 1993, he wrote *Roja* (The Rose, 1993), which became an instant hit and brought the promise of his creativity and craft to people's attention.

Simple but textured orchestration, innovative percussion and charming melodies create a unique feel in Rahman's songs. In no time, he was the Bombay film industry's favourite composer. Like R.D. Burman, he can deliver a trendy, modern track as easily as a folksy or traditional one.

Radha Kaise Na Jale for example, from *Lagaan* (Land Tax, 2001) is a listener's treat:

When Krishna meets all those women in the forest
of Madhuban
Now laughing, now naughty, now mischievous,
How can Radha not feel jealous?

The way Rahman effortlessly used elements of Indian classical music is something that would have made his predecessors Naushad and S.D. Burman truly proud. The song is visualised as a semi-classical Indian dance in which Krishna wonders what Radha has to be jealous of when he is spending time with the *gopis*.[9] In turn, and revealing her insecurities, Radha explains how she cannot help but be jealous, because after all, they are women. The irresistible rhythmic beat, the whirlwind rendering alternating with playful tempos, makes the entire track quite enchanting. Even the *Holi*[10] elements in the song are endearingly different from the other Holi songs present in countless Hindi film songs. And the musical arrangements caress Asha Bhosle's sensuous throat with a lover's gentleness. Erotic wit, elements of classical dance and music, fun and frolic – all are interwoven, creating an experience of simultaneous religious, cultural and artistic exuberance.

Throughout their exotic history, Hindi film songs have blended elements of religion, devotion, eroticism and adventure, in a manner unlike those featured in the cinema of any other culture.

Take, for instance, the title-song sequence from the film *Satyam Shivam Sundaram* (Truth, Holiness, Beauty, 1978):

God is Truth, Truth is Shiva, Shiva is Beauty
Get up and discover how bright the whole creation is

In this scene, lead actress Zeenat Aman, wearing only a thin and light muslin cloth over the sensual curves of her breasts, 'prays' to a phallus-shaped stone idol of lord Shiva. The entire scene is charged with an erotic tension that propels the narrative forward. The song is about how every moment of life is blissful, a constant celebration, if we are able to reach out to the beauty that lies within us all. The serene and philosophical lyrics allow the audience to experience Zeenat Aman's physicality at work with the phallic stone and experience no sense of guilt.

---

[9] *Gopis,* or cow-herding girls, were actually saints from an earlier birth, blessed to be reborn as local girls who would flock around the Lord and frolic harmlessly together.
[10] The Festival of Colours, held in spring.

BELOW: Detail of a six-sheet poster of **Khalnayak** (1993)

ABOVE: **Lagaan** (2001)
BELOW: **Satyam Shivam Sundaram** (1978)
BELOW LEFT/RIGHT: Booklet **Satyam Shivam Sundaram** (1978)

Unique genre
Despite film songs remaining within the domain of popular and mass art, it is remarkable that they can nonetheless be creations of the finest poetry. Lyricists such as Shailendra, Sahir Ludhianvi, Kaifi Azmi, Majrooh Sultanpuri and Shakeel Badayuni could write racy songs as easily as songs about longing, emptiness, defeat and loss. With the deft use of just a few words they also brought a variety of metaphors into the language, which, through several generations of humming, have now become an integral part of Indian thinking.

The melodious and powerful music of the composers Anil Biswas, Roshan, O.P. Nayyar, Naushad, S.D. Burman, Madan Mohan, Shankar Jaikishen, Salil Chaudhury, R.D. Burman, Laxmikant Pyarelal, Kayanji Anandji, Anu Malik, Jatin Lalit, Shankar Ehsan Loy and A.R. Rahman turned the poetry of these lyricists into countless classic songs. Through a rather curious collaboration of film-makers, lyricists, composers, singers and stars, Indian cinema developed a way of combining poetry, music and narrative into a unique genre that is found nowhere else in world cinema.

TAMIL CINEMA   THE SIGNIFICANT OTHER

BY: **SOUDHAMINI**

This book concentrates on the visual language of Hindi cinema. However, much of what is written here applies equally to India's other film cultures, whether Bengali, Assamese, Maharathi, Gujarati, Malayalam or any of the numerous film industries around the country. They do, of course, differ in their use of language and regional themes. Hindi cinema has one especially strong and independent competitor for its position as the Indian film culture most well-known and widely appreciated beyond the country's borders: the Tamil film industry. It has long been the most productive cinema culture in India, and is also the most flamboyant and expressive, with its authentic visual language. Here is the 'significant other'.

Anyone walking around Chennai for the first time will be struck by the huge billboards and hoardings advertising Tamil films lining many of the city's central avenues. Cinema is not only considered a traditional cultural form in Tamil Nadu, its heroes are demi-gods – definitely a few sizes larger than life! Many factors have contributed to the creation of this phenomenon.

First of all, Tamil culture is essentially expressive and celebratory by nature. Bright colours, loud gestures and spontaneous, untrammelled emotionalism mark social interaction – from the most intimate to casual and passing relationships. The food is filled with complex tastes, flowers are enjoyed as much for their colour as for their smell, and women wear them in profusion in their hair throughout the year. Ornamentation in gold, precious stones, silver, plastic or glass is common among women, and even men wear a lot of gold. It is a sensuous culture, which believes in demonstrating its emotions at all times, be they tragic, comic, aggressive, moralistic or even demonic.

All Tamil cultural forms, folk and classical, are highly developed. They involve make-up and colourful costumes, elaborate gesticulation of the hands, face and eyes, and intricate movements of the legs, hips and torso. The technology of cinema may have been invented in France, but in Tamil Nadu its aesthetics are derived directly from traditional art forms such as: *therukoothu*, folk theatre; *isai natakam*, musical theatre; *harikatha*, the oral storytelling tradition; and *silambattam*, a traditional martial art using sticks. In this respect, the fact that it is a regional cinema has helped, rather than hindered, its growth. Also, unlike cinema elsewhere in the country, it never split into two streams – mainstream commercial cinema and art, or 'parallel', cinema – and this allowed it to remained vibrant: exploring and exploding its limits *within* the mainstream matrix. Film hoardings are above all an expression of this celebratory performing instinct.

TOP: Rajinikanth
RIGHT/ABOVE: Tuticorin, Madurai and Chennai

ABOVE: Vijayakanth

Sitting cheek by jowl with film posters are the hoardings of politicians and political leaders. The late M.G. Ramachandran (M.G.R.), Tamil Nadu's former Chief Minister, is the most successful example of the actor-turned-politician in India. His protégée, and paramour in many films, J. Jayalalitha, is the present Chief Minister. The leader of the opposition is M. Karunanidhi, an aficionado of the Dravidian movement and chiefly instrumental in 'scripting' the image of the star-politician in Tamil cinema.

Before breaking up into rival factions, the Dravidian Progressive Party (DMK), with a rising sun as its symbol, was all set to usher in a new dawn in Tamil Nadu. It was a socio-cultural revolution that harnessed its primary propaganda organ, cinema, as its mouthpiece. All other existing cultural forms were community-specific and were enjoyed within a strict social hierarchy. Cinema arrived from overseas and the Dravidian movement quickly took hold of it and made it irrevocably its own. Hence, the larger-than-life film hoardings on the street are also part of the official state machinery in Tamil Nadu. The 'image' is not merely expressive and celebratory it is also rhetorical. It bursts at the seams with political messages and sub-texts.

Apparently, the propaganda wing of the Dravidian movement consciously fashioned the image of M.G.R. as a combination of Douglas Fairbanks and Rudolf Valentino, so as to capture the public imagination. He soon came to represent the archetype of the dashing young rebel, rising from the frayed margins of society to lead the people to power. He was known as much for his social conscience as his romantic charm and his fighting skills, which included sword fighting and *Silambattam*. He was simultaneously a son of the soil and a Western buccaneer. Most importantly, he was a construct.

ABOVE: MGR
RIGHT: Political party banners and paintings
BELOW: Sections of a mural in Chennai, depicting Tamil political and film history.

A third aspect of the larger-than-life image is related to the religious nature of Tamil culture. Long after the rest of the country ceased making *mythologicals* – the first genre of Indian cinema – Tamil cinema continued to produce them. Even in sitcoms on television today, gods and goddesses, young and old, fill the screen. Such representations necessarily require larger-than-life dimensions. So as well as being expressive and rhetorical, hoarding images are iconic.

Besides their aesthetic implications, mythologicals have ensured the development of state-of-the-art special-effects technology in the Tamil film industry. Films featuring actors playing two, three or even four roles are very much the fad. The latest craze to hit the Tamil screen is computer graphics, used particularly in song picturisations to uncanny effect. True Tamil cinema resembles films by George Méliès rather than the Lumière brothers.

Of course, it is not the only the image that is larger than life. The persona of the Tamil film hero has always had to fulfil many expectations. He must be highly expressive, multi-faceted and skilled in *sakala kala vallavan* (speech, combat and the arts). Additionally, he has to have an active social conscience, so even if he is not a politician he must still bear in mind that his actions must be for the greater good of his family, his community and his country. He must also be touched by the divine – or the demonic – for to remain merely human is hardly considered heroic.

At the same time, and this is important, he must be modest! Within the narrative of the film, the same larger-than-life hero is seen trying very hard to play Everyman. The glamour is in the packaging, the siren call that lures the passing traveller. Once the ticket is literally 'bought', the discourse shifts to identification. Everyman lives every day just like everyone else, distinguished only by a certain sense of style, a flamboyant approach, and a way with words, actions and gestures that is both fascinating and familiar – that ensnares the imagination.

own to advise fans on whom to vote for by making public announcements to his huge following.'

This constant interplay of image and reality, public persona and character is the double bind with which Tamil cinema mesmerises its audience and holds them in thrall to this day. The master of style in Tamil cinema today is 'Superstar' Rajnikant. Significantly, although he has never stood for elections himself, he has been known to advise fans on whom to vote for by making public announcements to his huge following. This can sway elections in Tamil Nadu.

ABOVE LEFT: MGR and Rajinikanth together on a political painting.
TOP RIGHT: **Agathiar** (1972)

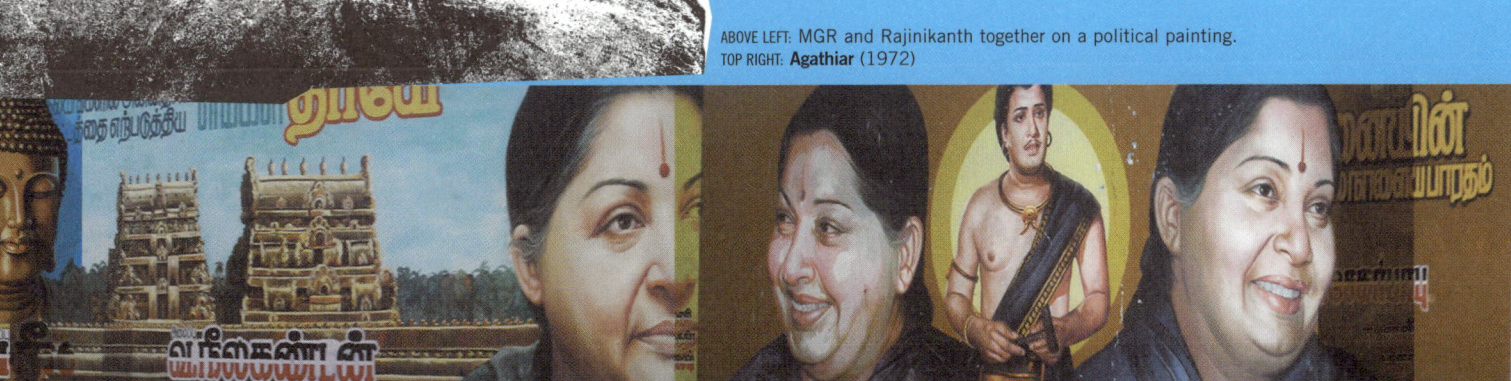
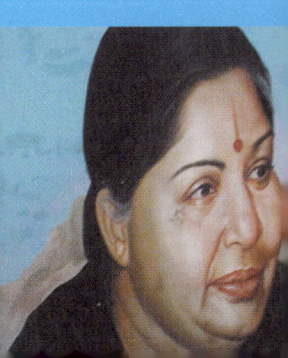

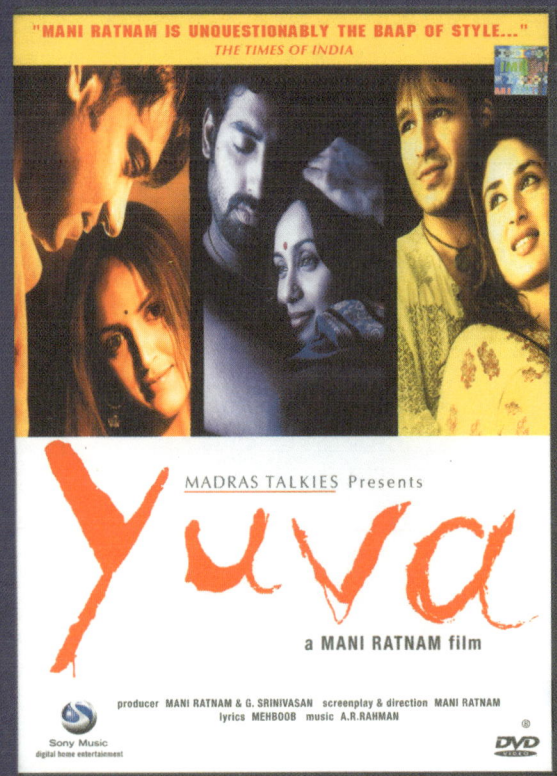

Similarly, a heroine's vitality plays a greater role than her glamour, because hidden in the Tamil collective consciousness is the blessed idea that the 'true' woman is one who can match her man in wit, valour, strength and compassion. An independent woman is defined as one who can hold her own in both domestic and wider social relationships. Therefore, although they are made within an essentially patriarchal structure, there have been strong portrayals of women in Tamil film.

Mani Ratnam's latest film was released in two versions, *Yuva* (*Youth,* 2003) in Hindi and *Ayutha Ezuthu* (*Youth,* 2004) in Tamil. There are two small but crucial differences between the final scenes of the two versions that may bring home the contrast in sensibilities between Hindi and Tamil cinema. *Yuva* ends with four young men who, having won the elections, enter the Assembly in exaggerated slow motion ready to take over the system. Their every gesture reeks of machismo and youthful arrogance. *Ayutha Ezutha* ends on quite a different note: here too the hero and his companions enter the political arena, but the hero's personality is much more individuated. He takes his seat modestly, he is merely a small man determined to do his bit. Equally significant is that of the four young leaders in the Tamil version, one is a girl!

Another strong female archetype is the mother. While the father is the authority figure, to be rebelled against when a tyrant, but emulated when benign, the mother is the emotional core of the social structure. In this respect, all of Indian cinema remains unified, and the mother figure is its central image.

In Tamil cinema the *word* dominates. Because of its sacred associations, language plays a crucial role in all aspects of Tamil culture. And with the accretion of political messages worked into film dialogues, the word becomes paramount. Mainly by way of the veterans C.N. Annadurai and M. Karunanidhi, political oratory and social rhetoric coalesced into strongly dramatic and oral texturing of the film medium itself. Long speeches involving complex arguments, considerable verbal rhymes, rich imagery and liberal use of local idioms and figures of speech, caused Tamil cinema to develop along the lines of the oral and performative arts, rather than the visual or lyrical arts. This is still the dominant flavour of Tamil films today. Even more than 'action', the oral element prevails. But it is as oral as Shakespeare is oral – and by that same measure, universal. All it requires is correct subtitling to communicate effectively.

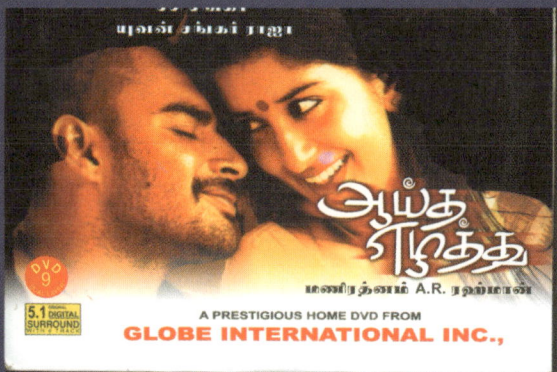

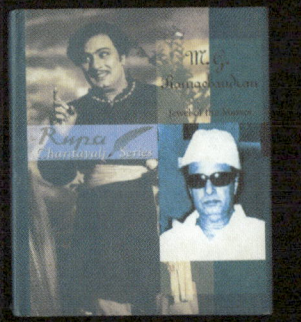
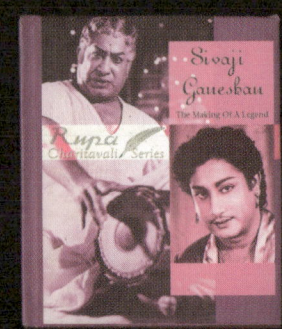

ABOVE: **Yuva** in Hindi and **Ayutha Ezuthu** in Tamil (2004).
BELOW: On the set of Mani Ratnam's film **Ayutha Ezuthu**.

TOP ROW: M. Karunanidhi, film credit and audio cassette.
ABOVE FROM LEFT TO RIGHT: Books featuring MGR, Sivaji Ganeshan and Kamalhasan, published by Rupa.

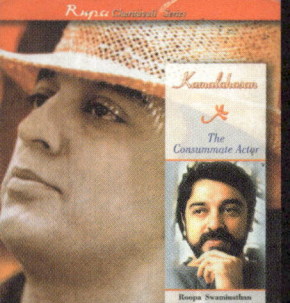

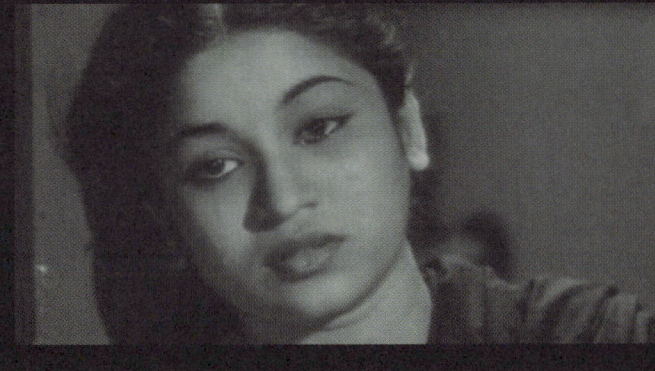

The highly melodramatic aspects of Tamil cinema, especially in the way pathos is expressed, may often alienate outsiders. It is a culture that even has a traditional lament, the *oppari,* a highly conventionalised, long, wailing song of mourning. To confuse matters further, after the *oppari* concludes and the body is being carried to the cemetery, drums are played, young men dance and firecrackers are let off. Celebration and tears are but two sides of the same coin – as are birth and death – and after the loss has been sufficiently mourned, the rejoicing begins for the soul's freedom from earthly bondage.

What is must be remembered in this context is that despite its strong basis in technology, Tamil cinema is still a 'rural' art form. Many directors come to Chennai from their native villages or small towns, only chasing the dream of making a film. When these films are made, their stories are set in rural scenery. Their sensibilities are rural and so are their target audiences. Very few films are really urban in their setting and sensibility. To watch Tamil cinema is to feel the pulse of the rural heartland. It is a window to the agrarian lifestyle, its folklore and belief systems.

ABOVE: **Arasilankumari** (1961)

Details of original hand-painted designs for posters by Sundar (Safire Printers).

Panama Pashama (1968)

Curiously, I believe it is in its humour that Tamil cinema is most inward looking. Its jokes are in-jokes. Film-makers love to play with dialects and idiosyncratic speech patterns within the dominant language. There is a lot of self-reflexive talk – about politics and current affairs, local and global, about film itself and about audiences. In these ways, it is unconsciously and un-selfconsciously modern. And this humour is contagious. Without necessarily understanding all the cultural nuances one can still relate to the sense of fun, the quick responses, the irreverence and the overriding sense of jubilance. In a manner reminiscent of Italian culture, family, food and fun dominate social interaction. Excess and abundance are signifiers of a generosity of spirit and of hospitality – another strong cultural marker. Strangers will always be made welcome in a Tamil landscape, be it physical or cultural.

Social dramas are still the dominant genre in Tamil cinema, whether they involve conflicts between generations, families, communities or clans. But where *izzat* (honour) seems to be the main bone of contention in Hindi cinema of the same genre, in Tamil films conflicts are usually based on emotional misunderstandings or property disputes. The ego is important but emotion even more so. In earlier times, such films seemed to express a belief in negotiated settlements, and sometimes even in the reformation of the villain, often a 'cousin'. Modern films seem to thrive on bloodthirsty, violent solutions. This, I believe, is because the distinct genres of the action film, thriller and romance do not really exist as in Tamil cinema. Audiences now being fed regularly with Hollywood action flicks dubbed into Tamil apparently expect similar performances from their own heroes. Or so it is believed. And it is the social drama that somehow has to provide a wide variety of 'thrills' within its loosely-structured narrative. So every social context for potential violence, particularly community differences, is exploited to the full.

TOP: **Dhool** (2003)
RIGHT: Details of original collages featuring the film star Rajinikanth. Designs by Sundar (Safire Printers).

The best entry point by far into Tamil cinema is through music, particularly that of A.R. Rahman, for he works predominantly with rhythm, which communicates universally. He came along at a time when 'fusion' was the buzzword – between Hindi and Tamil and between India and the West – and the quickest way to meld differences was to smother them with pulsating rhythm. It is interesting, however, that Tamil directors like Shankar, and choreographers like Prabhudeva, took this new beat to heart; creating amazing song picturisations whose motifs, settings, quirky characterisations and quick edits signified a fantasy landscape that was both familiar and new. They combined cyberspace with a village, bars and boardrooms with green fields, and college classrooms with Hungarian palaces and Samurai forts. And so we come full circle, from M.G.R. to A.R. Rahman, and see how the world enters Tamil cinema – and is made welcome.

TOP LEFT TO RIGHT: A.R. Rahman, Ilayaraja and Shankar
BELOW: Madurai

LEFT: MGR memorial, Marina Beach, Chennai.

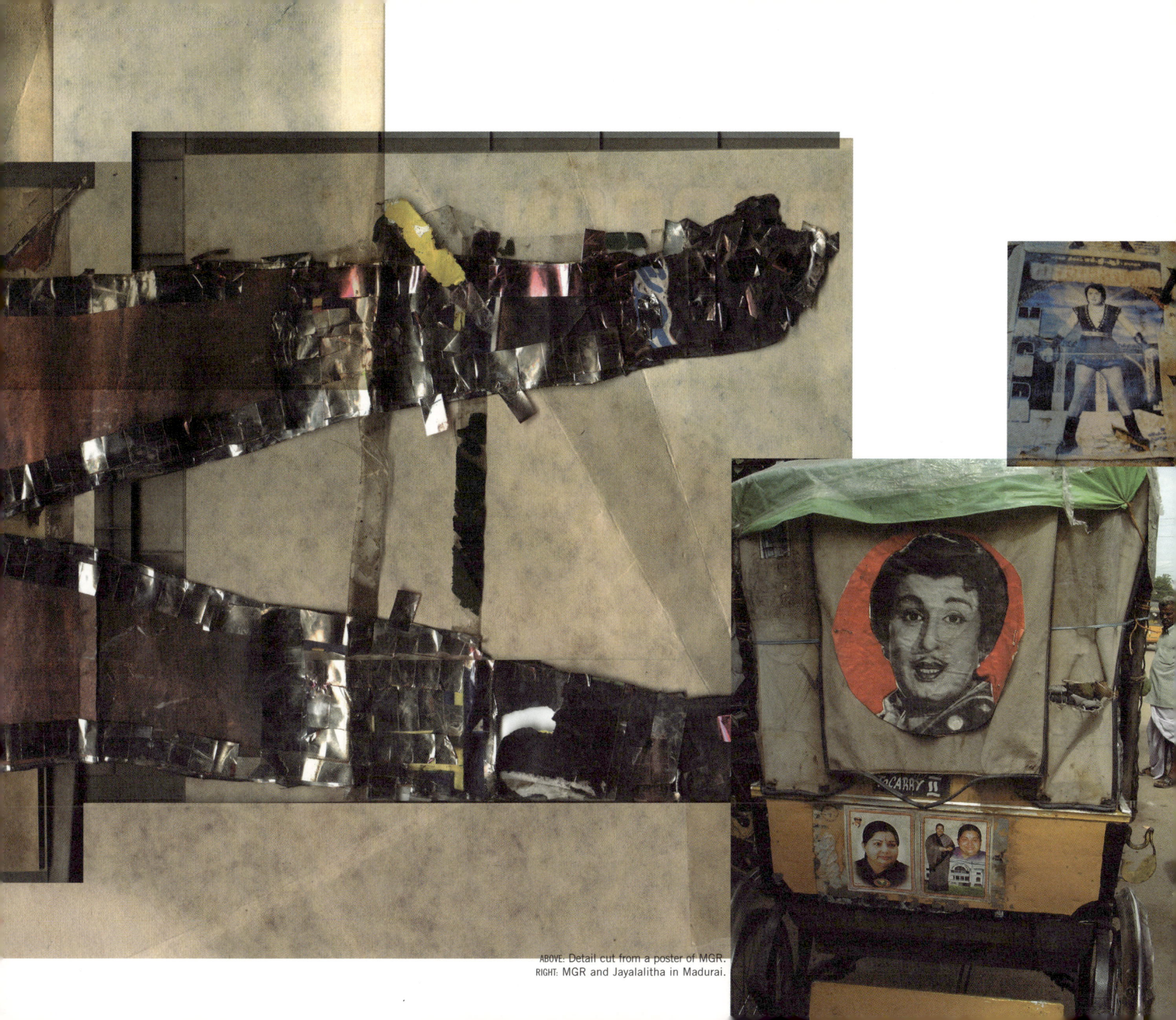

ABOVE: Detail cut from a poster of MGR.
RIGHT: MGR and Jayalalitha in Madurai.

The Mehboob Khan office and archive containing untouched classic posters, booklets and films from the past.

DISTRIBUTION

TOP: The manager worships Shirdi Sai Baba.
RIGHT: Projectionists screening a film in Naaz Cinema, Bombay.

Poster suppliers sell new and old posters or cards to cinemas for the promotion of new releases and reruns.

Urban film transport

Hindi films for rent in Iranian shop

IRAN AND HINDI CINEMA
STRONG BONDS
BY: HADI TEHRANI

India shares a cultural background with Iran that dates from long before Islam became the dominant religion there. It is therefore unsurprising that Iranian and Indian cinema should develop a special bond. Hindi film was greatly inspired by the formula and the stories of popular *Parsi* theatre plays,[1] and Iranian cinema was much influenced by early Indian cinema.

It was only in the 1930s that film-makers based in Iran started making films in India with the help of Indian directors and technicians. The first Iranian films were silent: classic love stories based on well-known Persian legends such as *Leili va Majnoun* (Leili and Majnoun, 1937, East India, Bombay), *Shirin va Farhad* (Shirin and Farhad, 1936, Empire Film, Bombay), *Chesmhaye Siah* (Black Eyes, 1935, Krishna Film, Bombay) and *Ferdowsi* (Ferdowsi, 1934, Empire Film, Bombay).
Iran's first film production with sound, *Dokhtare Lor* (Lor's Daughter, 1933, Empire Film, Bombay), was also made in India, by the Iranian director Abdolhossein Sepanta. It was only screened in Iran some years later.

Audiences from both nations could identify with each other's stories and acting styles. Especially during the reign of Shah Muhammad Reza Pahlavi (reign 1941–79), music and dance scenes were accepted as integral to Iranian cinema. In contrast to Hindi films, in which they were performed by groups, here they were performed by individuals.

Co-productions, which were made on a regular basis, include: *Homaie Saadat* (Lucky Dog, 1971) made in Iran with an Indian director, Fabi Chanakia; and *Mamoure Ma Dar Kerachi* (Our Agent in Karachi, 1973) directed by the Iranian Mohammad Reza Fazeli using Indian actors. It was easy for Iranian actors to find work in Hindi movies and for Indian actors to join the Iranian film industry.

Before the Iranian Islamic Revolution in 1979, Hindi cinema was screened in theatres there for everybody to enjoy. With the arrival of video in the 1980s, the popularity of Indian cinema grew rapidly. Posters and postcards featuring Indian actors appeared at markets and were collected by Iranian film lovers.
Following the revolution, Hindi films were banned because they contained songs and dances. If such films were shown at all, these and other forbidden scenes were cut.
This does not mean that Indian films are no longer to be seen, however. Original uncut films can still be bought on the black market, where they have escaped the attention of the censor board.
For many years, the Iranian film authorities were unable to deal with Hindi films, but they are now steadily appearing on the legal market, with covers featuring sales information and an image from the film.

Sources
A Guide to Iranian Cinema Directors 1930–1999, Sayyed Morteza Sayyed Mohammadi, Tehran, 1999.
A Guide to Iranian Cinema 1929–1971, Jamal Omid, Tehran, 1993.

[1] *Parsi* theatre: travelling companies run by Persians who had fled their homeland for religious reasons. Their performances are renowned for their romantic stories and comical interludes.

ABOVE: **Dokhtare Loor** (1933)
BELOW: Advertisement FilmFare (1954)

SOVIET FANS
INDIAN POPULAR CINEMA & SOVIET MOVIE ENTHUSIASTS
BY: SUDHA RAJAGOPALAN

Some of the earliest foreign audiences for Indian popular cinema were in the Soviet Union, and Indian films ran in packed movie-halls there between 1954 and 1991. The popularity of these films was legendary, and the subject of both serious debate and local humour in post-Stalinist Soviet society: a letter from a moviegoer to a film journal in the 1970s proclaimed that only a *yogi* could possibly endure the long queues for tickets to an Indian film show at a Soviet theatre! Audience members often commented that their theatres showed good, bad, and Indian films, because Indian popular cinema was perceived as a category unto itself. Clearly, it played a significant role in the Soviet popular culture and imagination of this period.

The early years

Soviet familiarity with Bombay melodramas began in the 1950s. The mood in Soviet society was sombre in the years after the Second World War. The problems associated with the reconstruction of industry and recuperation from the trials of war were exacerbated by the increasingly restrictive nature of Stalinist policies during this period. Foreign contact was circumscribed, and foreign films practically disappeared from Soviet screens. With the death of Stalin in 1953, the most repressive era in Soviet history drew to a close. The new leader, Khrushchev, launched the de-Stalinisation campaign in 1956, lifting some Stalinist measures and introducing a comparatively flexible state policy. The brief cultural and social revival that followed came to be known as 'the Thaw' in Soviet history.

Between the death of Stalin in 1953 and Khrushchev's de-Stalinisation speech in 1956, another landmark event contributed to the cultural reawakening in Soviet society: in 1954, the first Indian film festival was held in Moscow and other cities, and the films won adoring audiences across the Soviet Union. The festival's phenomenal success ensured the unabated import of Indian popular films, mainly from Bombay, until the end of the Soviet era.

With their flights of fantasy and frequent portrayals of individuals who take up causes and redress social wrongs, these films were a paradox in the authoritarian and ideologically grounded Soviet Union.[1]

The first popular Indian melodrama to be screened in Soviet theatres was *Awaara* (The Vagabond). Produced in 1951, it opened the Indian film festival in Moscow.

Soviet moviegoers were charmed by Indian melodramas, their accommodation of fantasy and dream sequences, the perceived flawless beauty of the stars and the novelty of the music and landscapes. Raised on socialist-realist films about war and revolution, viewers fondly recall these melodramas, which showed life as it was rather than the varnished reality portrayed in Soviet films. In contrast to domestic films that emphasised the public and the ideological, Indian films were personal stories with down-to-earth, familiar characterisations. In the perception of early Soviet audiences, another strength of Indian popular cinema was that it combined social issues with captivating music and sentimental romance. The turbulent emotions and trials of love were entertaining cinematic fare for a generation weary of war, and films about it. They were moved by the overt personal emotions displayed in Indian cinema. Furthermore, the female characterisations in these films were a refreshing alternative to representations of women as peasants and workers in Soviet art and cinema. In the words of one observer 'Indian popular films began the democratisation of Soviet society long before *perestroika* and *glasnost*.'

From the sixties to the eighties

By the early 1970s, Soviet film production had begun to diversify, resulting in more entertaining films. Additionally, an increasing number of films were being imported from the United States, France, Britain, countries of the socialist bloc and elsewhere. There were more blockbuster-hit films from India than any other foreign country in the Soviet Union in this period. On occasion, the number of Indian popular films in the charts surpassed even that of domestic productions. In these decades, Soviet film journals and newspapers

ABOVE: **Commando** (1988)
TOP RIGHT: **Apoorva Sahodarigal** (1983)
RIGHT: **Chandni** (1989)
BELOW: **Pyar ke Naam Qurban** (1990)

were inundated with fan mail from admirers of Indian popular films. Viewers declared in their letters that they were bored with domestic cinema, which dwelt on factory life and industrial production problems; such films 'prolong the working day' they complained. Many Soviet spectators observed that domestic cinema was about 'our problems' and explained that Indian films were appealing because they allowed viewers to forget those problems. Fans compared Indian films to *skazkas*, Russian fairy-tales; audiences could escape into a fantasy world – a construct that corresponded with their ideas about India.

The on-screen romance between Raj Kapoor and Nargis, as in *Awaara*, was something of a legend. But even viewers of later generations attributed the appeal of Indian films to their insistence on emphasising personal emotions such as love, faith and trust. Soviets did have access to domestic romantic films but these rarely ended fortuitously, and love stories were camouflaged in social themes.

In post-Stalinist society, Indian films were also admired because they were cathartic for the audience. Experts acknowledged that the melodramatic excesses of Indian film met viewers' emotional needs. Moviegoers' accounts of the reception of these productions are invariably peppered with statements like 'I cried throughout the film' and 'the entire audience wept for the heroes'. Many observers observed that the hardships endured by the protagonists in Indian films moved viewers to sympathetic tears, and helped them to dispel their many worries and forget their tedious workday.

Furthermore, at a time when opportunities for travel were confined to a select few, cinema in the Soviet Union was a means for fans to vicariously experience the pleasures of travel. Many praised Indian films for allowing them to experience a society and culture so far removed from their own mundane lives. For Soviet audiences, the special quality of these films was their exotic aesthetic. This exoticism lay in the scenes of India's landscapes and cultures, and in the perceived other-worldly beauty of its stars. The films were perceived as ethnographic texts and were seen to represent Indian culture in an unmediated fashion; they were said to transport viewers to India in their imaginations. Countless moviegoers were also inspired by films to engage professionally with India.

It was not only Indian cinema's many distinctive features that attracted Soviet filmgoers. People believed that India and the Soviet Union bore many similarities that facilitated audiences' identification with these films and their protagonists. To early viewers of films such as *Awaara*, they represented a world that seemed to share many of the Soviet Union's problems in the pre- and post-war eras. Before the Soviet Union embarked upon its industrialisation of the largely agrarian economy in the 1930s, illiteracy and poverty were commonplace. Indian films of the 1950s and 1960s demonstrated that similar challenges faced India as it threw off the shackles of colonial rule. Early viewers responded with sympathy to these issues raised in Indian popular cinema.

Soviet audiences also identified with the moral code of Indian films, and recognised aspects of their own lives in them. The absence of physical intimacy on screen met with the approval of most people. They were comfortable with Indian popular films because the portrayal of emotional rather than physical love made it possible to watch them with their families, who shared the films' moral assumptions. The importance of family and the sanctity of the parent–offspring relationship in Indian popular films struck a resonant chord with audiences of similar cultural backgrounds. The manner in which these relationships were portrayed differed from the approaches of both the Soviet and Western cinema to which they had access. Many admirers in the Soviet Union also found Indian popular cinema to be benevolent and humane, imparting 'correct' values, which they juxtaposed against the perceived aggression in films from the West. Some moviegoers suggested that they were raised with good and decent values, and Indian films enhanced the viewer's sense of appropriate behaviour.

There was clearly a cultural space in Soviet society for film enthusiasts who rejected overtly ideology-laden and politicised entertainment in favour of the world of Indian melodrama.

With the fall of the Soviet regime, the special relationship with India ended and foreign markets opened up; Indian films ceased to be screened in Soviet theatres. However, enthusiasts can now buy new Indian films on video within weeks of their release in India. Furthermore, post-Soviet Internet culture has created countless opportunities for fans to gather information, communicate with each other and gossip about their favourite Indian celluloid heroes. Soviet and post-Soviet audiences have proved resilient, and they have remained loyal to Indian popular film.

[1] The first two Indian films to be screened in Soviet theatres, in 1949 and 1951, were realist films about the Bengal famine and the partition of the subcontinent in the 1940s. They garnered a few critical reviews, but made little impact on the general movie audience.

Sources
This article draws on research conducted in Russia in 1998, 2001 and 2002 for a doctoral dissertation on the significance of Indian popular cinema in Soviet society. Materials used in this article include surveys, interviews, fans' letters to Soviet film journals and unpublished letters sent to film officials by movie enthusiasts.

ABOVE: **Mujrim** (1989)
RIGHT: **Tridev** (1989)

ABOVE AND RIGHT: Sha Rukh Khan on tour in the USA and Europe (2001). Photograph: Jon Page/Hyphen Films Collection.

THE BRANDING OF BOLLYWOOD

BY: NASREEN MUNNI KABIR

Indian films have been shown throughout the world during the last fifty years, and have become widely regarded as great and lively alternatives to Hollywood productions. They appeal not only to audiences of Indian origin, who have settled in every corner of the world, but also to Africans, Russians and Middle-Easterners.

These audiences of millions have grown up on Bombay movies with their larger-than-life heroes and perfectly adoring heroines. The characters populate multi-layered films lasting approximately two and a half hours that segue seamlessly between romance, action, suspense, crime and grand family sagas. Although the films are often formulaic, Indian cinema has produced its share of exceptional movies that have broken conventions, or created their own. *Awaara* is a prime example of these. Even though it was released in 1951, still today many older Chinese fondly recall and speak of the exuberance of this film directed by Raj Kapoor – he also starred in the film, alongside the celebrated actress Nargis. In Greece, Mehboob Khan's 1957 masterpiece, *Mother India*, was regarded as one of the most powerful Indian films of all time. It was so popular in Greece that two songs from it were re-recorded in Greek and were big hits there. Another Raj Kapoor film, *Sangam* (1964), still brings affectionate smiles to the faces of Iranians and Russians, for whom Indian cinema meant Raj Kapoor. While Western critics were enthralled by the brilliance of the Bengali films by Satyajit Ray, films made in the sister-languages Hindi and Urdu (collectively known as 'Hindi films') won over hordes of fans all over the world. A Turk will happily sing a favourite film song if asked; a young Russian woman may say that her role model is actress Hema Malini rather than Julia Roberts; a Moroccan will declare emphatically that A. R. Rahman is no less than a genius; the eyes of an Egyptian police officer will light up at the mention of India's biggest icon and star, Amitabh Bachchan; and an Indonesian teenager will jump for joy if she hears that a new Shah Rukh Khan movie is in town.

Monsoon Wedding (2001)

Conquering the West

This level of appreciation has not spread to the potentially vast white European audiences, in spite of Indian cinema being featured at several film festivals in Europe since the mid-eighties, and broadcast regularly on television – for instance on Channel 4 in the United Kingdom. If mentioned at all, Indian movies were usually dismissed as 'dreadfully long love stories with lots of singing and dancing'.

A change in attitude towards Indian popular cinema in the West began in Britain in the late 1990s, demonstrating the increasing influence of the Asian community on mainstream British culture. Asian comedies on the BBC, and the popularity of Indian cuisine, fashion and *Bhangra* music are further examples of this phenomenon. By this time, the Asian Diaspora had grown in numbers and affluence. By 2002, the 'brown pound' had become a significant economic force, and catalysed new activities. Andrew Lloyd Webber's stage musical *Bombay Dreams* opened in London and was sold on its promise of offering the delights of Bollywood. Although reviews were mixed, the musical ran successfully for two years until closing in June 2004.

The term 'Bollywood' was coined for the first time in the 1980s in an attempt to express a link between Bombay production and Hollywood's impact and size, but is still considered patronising and simplistic by many Indian film-makers. The Bollywood influence is also evident in a number of cinema and television advertisements. *Lagaan* (Land Tax, 2001), the Oscar-nominated film much loved by the white audiences who saw it in limited numbers, received a good deal of attention in the press. The success of Mira Nair's *Monsoon Wedding* (2001), particularly in the USA, and Gurinder Chadha's British production, *Bend it like Beckham* (2002), made Indian entertainment appealing and acceptable. It seemed that the West had suddenly fallen in love with all things Indian.

Bollywood/Hollywood (2002)

'*A change in attitude towards Indian popular cinema in the West began in Britain in the late 1990s, demonstrating the increasing influence of the Asian community on mainstream British culture.*'

Aishwarya Rai in **Bride and Prejudice** (2004)

Bombay Dreams (2004)

LEFT: Amitabh Bachchan, commercial
BELOW: Soap powder commercial set at a *Holi* celebration in the film **Baaghban**.

Amitabh Bachchann, commercial for an ayurvedic medicine.

LEFT: Shah Rukh Khan, commercial for cars.

LEFT: Aishwarya Rai, advertisement for jewellery.
ABOVE: Amir Khan, advertisement for watches.

Obsessed by Bollywood

In India too, popular films were considered largely escapist fare until the early 1990s when the middle-classes, who had loved the Indian movies of the fifties and sixties, returned in great numbers to the cinema. Other important developments were the club scene's embracing of Hindi film music and the mushrooming of television, cable and satellite channels. The now sixty-odd Indian television channels depend on Bollywood stars and movie clips to boost their ratings. India has become obsessed with Bollywood, and media reports on the lives of its A-list celebrities are no longer confined to film magazines; they feature daily in every Indian broadsheet. This fixation has led to other art forms in India being overshadowed. It is, for example, almost startling to see the leading quality newspaper, *The Times of India*, using Bollywood film titles as headlines to its analysis of the impact of the 2004 fiscal budget. Bollywood movies and imagery are used to communicate to the billion-strong population in all areas of everyday life. Bollywood is considered as cool in India as it is beyond its shores, and celebrating it has become a global affair.

Indian film has of course long enjoyed a worldwide audience of at least two billion. However, unless audiences in the West develop a sustained love for the films themselves, and not just the world of Bollywood, with its glamorous stars and spellbinding songs and dances, it is difficult to believe that their interest in Indian cinema is more than a passing fad.

B4U bollywood movie channel website

MTV India website

ABOVE: Amitabh Bachchan in the Royal Tropical Institute in Amsterdam, the Netherlands

Obsessed by Bollywood

In India too, popular films were considered largely escapist fare until the early 1990s when the middle-classes, who had loved the Indian movies of the fifties and sixties, returned in great numbers to the cinema. Other important developments were the club scene's embracing of Hindi film music and the mushrooming of television, cable and satellite channels. The now sixty-odd Indian television channels depend on Bollywood stars and movie clips to boost their ratings. India has become obsessed with Bollywood, and media reports on the lives of its A-list celebrities are no longer confined to film magazines; they feature daily in every Indian broadsheet. This fixation has led to other art forms in India being overshadowed. It is, for example, almost startling to see the leading quality newspaper, *The Times of India*, using Bollywood film titles as headlines to its analysis of the impact of the 2004 fiscal budget. Bollywood movies and imagery are used to communicate to the billion-strong population in all areas of everyday life. Bollywood is considered as cool in India as it is beyond its shores, and celebrating it has become a global affair.

Indian film has of course long enjoyed a worldwide audience of at least two billion. However, unless audiences in the West develop a sustained love for the films themselves, and not just the world of Bollywood, with its glamorous stars and spellbinding songs and dances, it is difficult to believe that their interest in Indian cinema is more than a passing fad.

B4U bollywood movie channel website

MTV India website

ABOVE: Amitabh Bachchan in the Royal Tropical Institute in Amsterdam, the Netherlands

Indian Fashion in Paris

REVIEW

BY: MARIJKE DE VOS

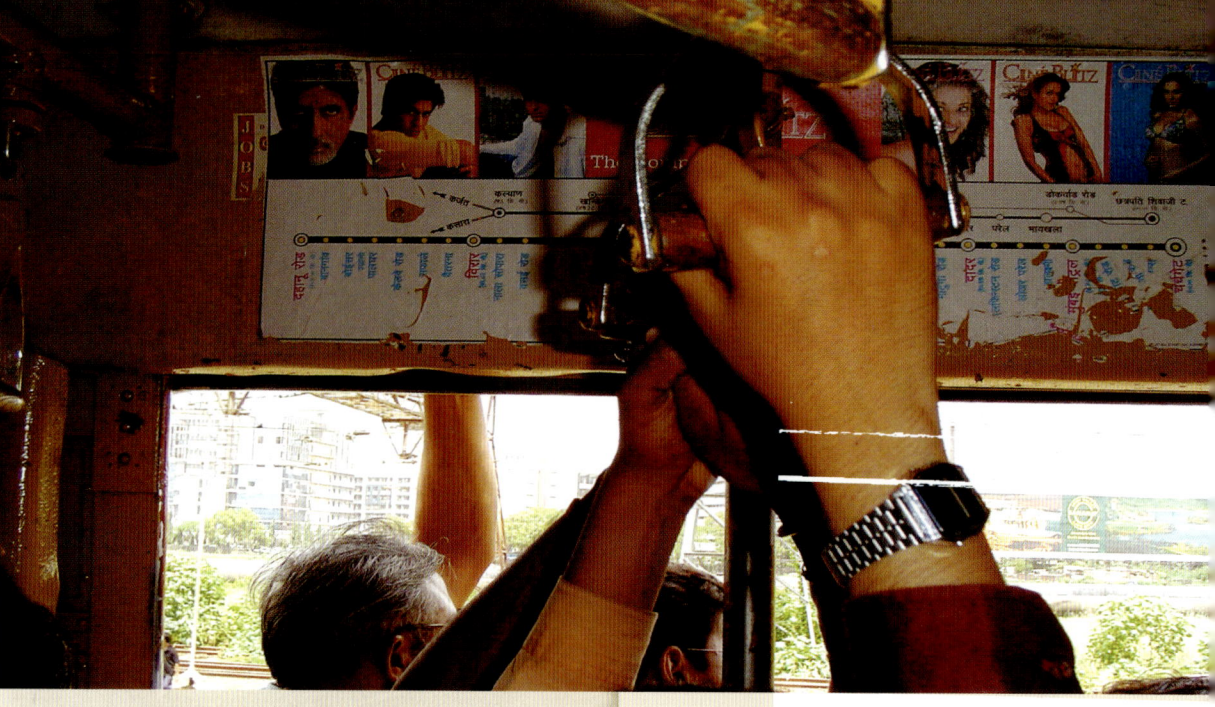

ABOVE: *CineBlitz* advertisements in a Bombay train.
BELOW: Shah Rukh Khan receiving Best Actor Award 2005.
Rani Mukherji receiving Best Actress Award 2005.

Critics

With the increasing role of the Internet as an open platform for an international audience to discuss films, Hindi cinema has received a substantial amount of both positive and negative criticism and reviews. The critics are straightforward in their approval or disapproval.

Traditionally, critical reviews were published in daily newspapers like *The Hindu*, *The Indian Express* and *The Times of India*. However, in-depth articles on popular films were rare. Film scholars ignored commercial Hindi films in favour of independent 'art movies'. Serious film magazines tended to look back into the past, and discussed films of the fifties or seventies from a social perspective. Glossy magazines such as *Filmfare*, *Cineblitz* and many others had a different agenda and concentrated on any subject relating to the stars, ignoring the storyline and characters. Music and songs, on the other hand, have always received serious and detailed reviews, both in film magazines and on the Internet.

Audiences

By the mid-1980s, middle-class audiences had deserted cinema halls. Films that featured excessive violence, gangsters, rape scenes and suchlike dominated the screen. This changed dramatically with the arrival of 'family' films directed by Sooraj Barjatya – in particular *Hum Aapke Hain Kaun* (Who Am I to You, 1994). The emphasis on the family struck a chord with India's rapidly growing middle class, with children studying in the West and with educated women who wanted a different kind of film – one that featured characters and situations they could readily identify with. Modernity and consumerism had made inroads into Indian society. With them came a fond nostalgia for the days of festivals and ceremonies shared by a joyful joint family, in which each person had his or her own role.

In 1993, the country was shaken by communal riots in Bombay. The Bombay film world was shocked that such events could occur in their free and liberal city, where for many years mixed couples had set the example for a secular modern India.

Mani Ratnam, the famous director from Tamil Nadu, made a controversial, but realistic, commercial film called *Bombay* (1995) about the riots there. It was the first step towards confronting mass audiences with conflict situations in a commercial setting.

Ratnam also set a high standard with his camera work, lighting and editing. He worked with the cameramen Rajiv Menon, Santosh Sivan and Ravi K. Chandran, and discovered the composer A.R. Rahman. They became the most sought-after talents in the Bombay film industry. Technically, films improved greatly from this period onwards. Thematically, a varied range of subjects surfaced. New genres – family films, erotic films, suspense and horror – were explored, and traditional genres reappeared in new guises. Films like the critically acclaimed 'social' *Black* (2005) by Sanjay Leela Bhansali, or 'patriotic' films like *Swades* (The Homeland, 2004) and *Lagaan* (Land Tax, 2001) by Ashutosh Gowarikar were far-removed from old stereotypes.

BELOW: Rani & Amitabh Bachchan in **Black** (2005)

BELOW: **Swades** (2004)

149

Box office

The opening up of the country to international markets in the early 1990s, and a growing community of NRIs (Non-Residential Indians) living in the West but still watching and buying Hindi films, influenced a change in content and visual style of new Hindi cinema. Fast edits and global settings, in which homosexuality and suicide are at least casually mentioned, as in *Kal Ho Na Ho* (Tomorrow may Never Come, 2003), helped to create something very different from the traditional Hindi film. Some films, including *Kal Ho Na Ho*, were shot entirely outside India. The phenomenon of the 'all-India film', that appealed to rural and urban populations, literate as well as illiterate audiences, has become weak and fragmented. The box office has split the Hindi film audience into factions, and films are rated as hits or flops according to how they fare in the distinct markets into which Indian film is divided: multiplexes in big cities (Bombay, Delhi, Kolkata, Bangalore, Chennai); cities; sub-territories such as Rajasthan and Bihar; and overseas territories, especially Britain and the USA.

Awards

The national government finally started taking the film industry seriously in 2002. Producers can now receive loans from the IDBI (Industrial Development Bank of India), which has at last recognised the film business as an official industry. Other banks and companies have also started investing in films. Since this policy shift, the need to accept money from unofficial sources has obviously decreased. This change was brought about primarily by a more professional approach by the dream merchants themselves. The younger generation of film-makers is better organised and more internationally oriented – able to keep their accounts and appointments. Another reason for this development is the vast and lucrative overseas market. Although most films still fail at the box office, film-making has developed into a potentially profitable business rather than an obscure money-wasting hobby.

A government board bestows the National Award on the best film, best actor and actress and so forth. These prizes are carefully distributed among India's many regional film industries, and are usually presented to non-commercial 'art films'. The Bombay film industry has the *Filmfare* Awards, which is organised by the Indian glossy magazine of the same name. These are awarded only to commercial films. In 2000, a third award was initiated, the IIFA (International Indian Film Academy) Awards. The annual ceremony is held outside India, has a high commercial profile and is intended as a meeting place for foreign exchange and interaction. The main focus is on television and the Internet. After members of the film industry have voted, the international audience is invited to participate by voting in web polls.

LEFT/ABOVE: **Kal Ho Na Ho** (2003)

Kal Ho Na Ho (2003)

Song Translations

Original song lyrics in order of appearance:

Street Singer
Babul Mora (O My Father, 1938)

*Babul Mora Naihar Chooto Hi Jaye
Chaar Kahar Mile, Doliya Sajaaye
Are Apna Begana Chooto Ja*

*Angna To Par Ghar Bhayo,
Dehri Bhayee Bides
Le Babul Ghar Aapno
Main Chali Piya Ke Des*

Awaara
Awaara Hoon (I Am a Vagabond, 1951)

*Awaara Hoon, Ya Gardish Mein Hoon
Aasman Ka Tara Hoon
Awaara Hoon*

*Ghar Baar Nahin Sansar Nahin
Mujhse Kisi Ko Pyaar Nahin
Us Paar Kisise Milne Ka Iqraar Nahin
Mujhse Kisi Ko Pyaar Nahin
Anjaan Nagar Sunsan Dagar Ka Pyara Hoon
Awaara Hoon*

*Abaad Nahin Barbaad Sahi
Gata Hoon Khushi Ke Geet Magar
Zakhmon Se Bhara Seena Hai Mera
Hansti Hai Magar Yeh Mast Nazar
Duniya Main Tere Teer Ka
Ya Taqdeer Ka Maara Hoon
Awaara Hoon*

Kaagaz Ke Phool
Waqt Ne Kiya Kya Haseen Sitam (How Time Has Caught Us, 1959)

*Waqt Ne Kiya Kya Haseen Sitam
Tum Rahe Na Tum Ham Rahe Na Ham
Waqt Ne Kiya*

*Beqaraar Dil Is Tarha Mile
Jis Tarha Kabhi Hum Juda Na The
Tum Bhi Kho Gaye, Hum Bhi Kho Gaye
Ek Raah Par Chalke Do Qadam
Waqt Ne Kiya*

*Jaayenge Kahan Sujhta Nahi
Chal Pade Magar Raasta Nahi
Kya Talaash Hai Kuchh Pata Nahin
Bun Rahe Hain Dil Khwaab Dum-Ba-Dum
Waqt Ne Kiya*

Taxi Driver
Jaaen To Jayen Kahan (Where Do I Go?, 1954)

*Jaen To Jaen Kahan
Samajhega Kaun Yahan
Dard Bhare Dil Ki Zuban*

*Mayuusiyon Ka Majama Hai Ji Mein
Kya Rah Gaya Hai Is Zindagi Mein
Ruh Mein Gam Dil Mein Dhuan …
Apana Bhi Gam Hai Unaka Bhi Gam Hai
Ab Dil Ke Bachaneki Ummeed Kam Hai
Ek Hai Kashti Sau Toofan …*

Pyaasa
Jaane Woh Kaise Log (Who Were Those?, 1957)

*Isko Hi Jeena Kehte Hain To Yunhi Ji Lenge
Uf Na Karenge, Lab See Lenge, Aansoo Pee Lenge
Gham Se Ab Ghabraana Kaisa Gham Sau Baar Mila …*

Mother India
Duniyan Mein Hum Aye Hain (We Were Born Never to Give Up, 1957)

*Duniyan Mein Hum Ayen Hain To Jeena Hi Padega
Jeevan Hai agar Zahar To Peena Hi Padega*

*Gir Gir Ke Museebat Mein Sambhalte Hi Rahenge
Jal Jaaye Magar Aag Pe Chalte Hi Rahenge
Gam Jisne Diya Hai Wahi Gam Door Karega*

and

*Aurat Hai Wo Aurat Jise Duniyan Ki Sharam Hai
Sansaar Mein Bas Laaj Hi Naari Ka Dharam Hai
Zinda Hai Jo Izzat Se Wo Izzat Se Marega …*

Mother India
O Jaane Walo (Those of You Who Are Going Away, 1957)

*O Jaane Walon Na Jaao Apna Ghar Chod Kar
Maata Bula Rahi Hai Tumhein Haath Jodkar*

*Nagari Ye Tumhari Galiyan Ye Tumhare Ye Tumhari Hai Bastiyan
Ujadi Hai Lakh Phir Bhi Hai Dharti Tumhari Maa …*

Teesri Manzil
O Haseena Zulfon Wali (O You Beauty with Lustrous Tresses, 1966)

*Wo Anjaana Dhoondhati Hoon, Wo Deewana Dhoondati Hoon
Jalakar Jo Chup Gaya Hai, Wo Parwana Dhoondati Hoon*

and

*O Hassena Zulfon Wali Jaane Jahaan
Dhoondhati Hai Qatil Aankhen Kiska Nishan …*

Mughal-e-Azam
Pyar Kiya To Darna Kiya (What's There to Fear about Being in Love?, 1960)

*Ishq Mein Jeena Ishq Mein Marna
Parda Nahin Jab Koi Khuda Se
Bandon Se Parda Karna Kya?*

Hum Dono
Abhee Naa Jaoo Chhodakar (Don't You Go Just Yet, 1961)

Abhi Na Jaao Chodakar, Ke Dil Abhi Bharaa Nahin

*Abhi Abhi To Aayee Ho, Bahaar Ban Ke Chhaayee Ho
Hawaa Zaraa Mahak To Le, Najar Jaraa Bahak To Le
Ye Shaam Dhal To Le Zaraa, Ye Dil Sanbhal To Le Zaraa
Mai Thodee Der Jee To Lun, Nashe Ke Ghoont Pee To Lun
Abhi To Kuchh Kahaa Nahin, Abhi To Kuchh Sunaa Nahin*

Chaudvin Ka Chand
Chaudvin Ka Chand Ho (Are You A Full Moon?, 1960)

*Chaudvin Ka Chand Ho, Ya Aftaab Ho
Jo Bhi Ho Tum Khuda Ki Kasam, Lajawaab Ho …
Zulfein Hain Jaise Kaandhe Pe Baadal Jhuke Hue
Aankhen Hain Jaise Maey Ke Pyaale Bhare Hue
Masti Hai Jisme Pyaar Ki Tum, Woh Sharaab Ho
Chaudvin Ka Chand Ho …*

*Chehra Hai Jaise Jheel Mein Khilta Hua Kanwal
Ya Zindagi Ke Saaz Pe Chhedi Hui Ghazal
Jaane Bahaar Tum Kisi Shayar Ka Khwaab Ho
Chaudvin Ka Chand Ho…*

Prem Pujari
Foolon Ke Rang Se (In the Colours of the Flowers, 1970)

*Tere Hi Sapne Lekar Ke Soya, Teri Hi Yaadon Mein Jaga
Tere Khayalon Mein Ulajha Raha Yun Jaise Ke Mala Mein Dhaga*

*Badal Bijali Chandan Pani, Jaisa Apana Pyaar
Lena Hoga Janam Humein Kaee Kaee Baar
Itana Madir, Itana Madhur Tera Mera Pyaar
Lena Hoga Janam Humein Kaee Kaee Baar*

Hare Rama Hare Krishna
Dum Maro Dum (Let's Get Stoned on Pot, 1971)

*Duniya Ne Humko Diya Kya
Duniya Se Humne Liya Kya
Hum Sabki Parwah Karen Kyon
Sabne Humara Kiya Kya*

Umrao Jaan
In Aankhon Ki Masti (My Intoxicating Eyes, 1981)

*In Ankhon Ki Masti Ke Mastane Hazaron Hain
In Ankhon Se Vaabastaa Afasaane Hazaaron Hain …*

*Ik Tum Hi Nahin Tanha, Ulafat Men Meri Rusava
Is Shahar Mein Tum Jaise Divane Hazaron Hain …*

*Is Shamm-E-Faroza Ko Andhi Se Darate Ho
Is Shamm-E-Farozaa Ke Paravane Hazaron Hain*

Khalnayak
Choli Ke Peeche Kya Hai (What's There under Your Blouse?, 1993)

*Choli Ke Peechhe Kya Hai …
Choli Mein Dil Hai Mera
Ye Dil Main Doongi Apne Ram Ko*

Lagaan
Radha Kaise Na Jale (How Can Radha Not Be Jealous?, 2001)

*Madhuban Mein Jo Kanhaiyya Kisi Gopi Se Mile
Kabhi Muskaye Kabhi Chede Kabhi Paat Kare
Radha Kaise Na Jale*

Satyam Shivam Sundaram
Satyam Shivam Sundaram (Truth, Godliness and Beauty, 1978)

*Ishwar Satya Hai, Satya Hi Shiv Hai, Shiv Hi Sundar Hai
Jaago Uth Kar Dekho, Jeevan Jyot Ujaagar Hai
Satyam Shivam Sundaram*

FILM INDEX

A
Aag (Fire, Raj Kapoor, H, 1948) 67
Aah (Sigh, Raja Nawathe, H, 1953) 17
Agathiar (Agasthya, A.P. Nagarajan, Tamil, 1972) 121
Aks (The Reflection, Rakesh Mehra, H, 2001) 83
Alam Ara (The Light of the World, Ardeshir Irani, H/Urdu, 1931) 61, 103
Amar Akbar Anthony (Amar, Akbar and Anthony, Manmohan Desai, H, 1977) 14, 56
Andaz (Nuance, Mehboob Khan, H, 1949) 106
Anubhav (Consciousness, Basu Bhattacharya, H, 1971) 85
Anuradha (Love of Anuradha, Hrishikesh Mukherjee, H, 1960) 85
Apoorva Sahodarigal (Unique Brothers, R. Thyagarajan, Tamil, 1983) 138
Aradhana (Aradhana, Shakti Samanta, H, 1969) 108, 112
Arasilankumari (A.S.A. Sami, Tamil, 1961) 123
Awaara (Vagabond, Raj Kapoor, H, 1951) 17, 65, 106, 138, 139, 141, 155
Ayutha Ezuthu (Youth, Mani Ratnam, Tamil, 2004) 122

B
Baharen Phir Bhi Aayengi (The Spring Will Return, Shaheed Latif, H, 1966) 25
Baaghban (The Guardian, Ravi Chopra, H, 2003) 40, 45, 144
Barsaat (Rain, Raj Kapoor, H, 1948) 106
Bazaar (K. Amarnath, H, 1949) 85
Bazaar (Sagar Sarhadi, H, 1982) 106
Bandini (Bandini, Bimal Roy, H, 1963) 76
Biwi Ho To Aisi (The Perfect Wife, J.K. Bihari, H, 1988) 85
Black (Sanjay Leela Bhansali, H, 2005) 148, 149
Bend it like Beckham (Gurinder Chadha, E, 2002) 143
Bobby (Raj Kapoor, H, 1973) 19
Bollywood/Hollywood (Deepa Mehta, E, 2002) 143
Bombay (Mani Ratnam, Tamil/H/Telugu, 1995) 148
Bride and Prejudice (Gurinder Chadha, E, 2004) 143

C
Chesmhaye Siah (Black Eyes, Abdolhossein Sepenta, silent, 1936) 137
Chandni (Moonlight, Yash Chopra, H, 1989) 138
Chaudhvin Ka Chand (The 14th Day of the Moon, M. Sadiq, H, 1960) 111
Chori Chori (Secretly, Anant Thakur, H, 1956) 85
Commando (B.Subhash, H, 1988) 138

D
Daag (Stigma, Amiya Chakravarty, H, 1952) 66
Deewaar (The Wall, Yash Chopra, H, 1975) 25, 59, 115
Deewaar (The Wall, Luthria, H, 2004) 96, 97
Devdas (Devdas, P.C. Barua, Benhali/H, 1935) 67, 103
Devdas (Devdas, Bimal Roy, H, 1955) 31, 76, 79
Devdas (Devdas, Sanjay Leela Bhansali, H, 2002) 62, 79
Dil (The Heart, Indra Kumar, H, 1990) 69
Dil Chahta Hai (What the Heart Desires, Farhan Akhtar, H, 2003) 69
Dil Deke Dekho (Give Me Your Heart, Nasir Hussain, H, 1959) 67
Dil Hai Ki Manta Nahin (The Heart Never Listens, Mahesh Bhatt, H, 1991) 85
Dil Se (From the Heart, Mani Ratnam, H, 1998) 98
Dil Tera Diwana (My Heart is Crazy About You, B.R. Panthulu, H, 1962) 108
Dilwale Dulhaniya Le Jayenge (The Brave Heart Takes Away the Bride, Aditya Chopra, H, 1995) 88
Do Bigha Zamin (Two Acres of Land, Bimal Roy, H, 1953) 95
Doctor (Phani Majumdar, H, 1940) 84
Dokhtare Lor (Lor's Daughter, Abdolhossein Sepanta, Persian, 1933) 137
Do Raaste (Two Roads, Raj Khosla, H, 1969) 82
Dushman (The Enemy, Nitin Bose, Bengali/H, 1938) 54, 103

E
Ek Duje Ke Liye (For Each Other, K. Balachander, H, 1980) 112
Evening in Paris, An (Shakti Samanta, H, 1967) 69, 71, 108

F
Ferdowsi (Ferdowsi, Abdolhossein Sepenta, silent, 1934) 137
Fida (Devotion, Ken Ghosh, H, 2004) 55

G
Gadar (Traitor, Anil Sharma, H, 2001) 96
Ghungroo ki Aawaaz (The Sound of Dancing Bells, Tulsi/Shyam Ramsay, H, 1981) Cover
Gold Medal, The (Ravi Nagaich, H, 1975) 19, 25
Gone with the Wind (Victor Fleming, E, 1939) 17
Gumrah (Lost, B.R. Chopra, H, 1963) 89
Gunsundari (Proper, Chandulal Shah, H, 1934) 82

H
Haqeeqat (Truth, Chetan Anand, 1964) 96
Hare Rama Hare Krishna (Dev Anand, H, 1971) 112, 155
Hawas (Desire, Karan Razdan, H, 2004) 55, 57
Hero (Subhash Ghai, H, 1983) 19
Hindustani (The Indian, Shankar, H/Tamil, 1996) 57, 96
Homaie Saadat (Lucky Dog, Fabi Chanakia, Farsi, 1971) 137
Howrah Bridge (Shakti Samanta, H, 1958) 106
Hum Aapke Hain Kaun? (Who Am I To You?, S. Barjatya, H, 1994) 86, 88, 148
Hum Dil De Chuke Sanam (I've Already Given My Heart, Sanjay Leela Bhansali, H, 2000) 89
Hum Dono (The Two of Us, Amarjeet, H, 1961) 111, 155
HumTum (Me–You, Kunal Kohli, H, 2004) 69

I
Insaan (Human Being, Narendra Bedi, H, 1982) 19
It Happened One Night (Frank Capra, E, 1934) 85

J
Jewel Thief (Vijay Anand, H, 1967) 108
Jis Desh Mein Ganga Behti Hai (The Land Where the Ganges Flows, Radhu Karmakar, H, 1960) 14
Jism (Body, Amit Saxena, H, 2003) 55
Junglee (The Savage, Subodh Mukherjee, H, 1961) 67

K
Kaagaz Ke Phool (Paper Flowers, Guru Dutt, H, 1959) 106, 107, 155
Kabhi Khushi Kabhie Gham (Sometimes Happiness, Sometimes Sorrow, Karan Johar, H, 2001) 40, 45, 88
Kal Ho Na Ho (Tomorrow May Never Come, Nikhil Advani, H, 2003) 84, 87, 150, 151
Kaliya Mardan (The Slaying of the Snake, Dadasaheb Phalke, silent, 1919) 39, 92
Kapaal Kundala (Kapaalkundala, Nitin Bose/Phani Majumdar, H, 1939) 103
Kashmir Ki Kali (The Flower of Kashmir, Shakti Samanta, H, 1964) 54, 69
Karma (Duty, J.L. Freer Hunt, E/H, 1933) 37
Khalnayak (The Villain, Subhash Ghai, H, 1993) 82, 116, 155
Khuddaar (Self-controlled, Ravi Tandon, H, 1982) 88
Kismet (Destiny, Gyan Mukherjee, H, 1943) 37, 85
Kohinoor (S.U. Sunny, H, 1960) 101
Kranti (The Revolution, Manoj Kumar, H, 1980) 19
Krantiveer (The Hero of the Revolution, Mehul Kumar, H, 1994) 96
Kunkul Duniya Na Maane (The Unexpected, V. Shantaram, Marathi/H, 1937) 85

L
Lagaan (Land Tax, Ashutosh Gowarikar, H, 2001) 54, 76, 92, 116, 117, 143, 148, 155
Lakshya (The Objective, Farhan Akhtar, H, 2004) 96
Lal Patthar (Red Stone, Sushil Majumdar, H, 1971) 88
Legend of Bhagat Singh, The (Rajkumar Santoshi, H/Bengali/Punjabi/E, 2002) 93
Leili va Majnoun (Leili and Majnoun, Abdolhossein Sepenta, silent, 1937) 137
Love in Tokyo (Pramod Chakraborty, H, 1966) 68
Love Story (Rajendra Kumar, H, 1981) 112
Love & God (K. Asif, H, 1986) 91

M
Madhumati (Madhumati, Bimal Roy, H, 1958) 91
Mahal (The Palace, Kamal Amrohi, H, 1949) 106
Maine Pyaar Kiya (I Fell In Love, S. Barjatya, H, 1989) 88
Mamoure Ma Dar Kerachi (Our Agent in Karachi, Mohammad Reza Fazeli, Persian, 1973) 137
Main Hoon Na (It Is Not Me, Farah Khan, H, 2004) 35
Mangalsutra (B. Vijay, H, 1981) 14
Monsoon Wedding (Mira Nair, H/E, 2001) 88, 142, 143
Mother India (Mehboob Khan, H, 1957) 17, 59, 76, 90, 95, 106, 107, 141, 155
Mr. India (Shekhar Kapur, H, 1987) 96
Mughal-e-Azam (The Great Moghul, K. Asif, Urdu, 1960) 54, 59, 110, 155
Mujrim (Accused, Umesh Mehra, H, 1989) 139
Murder (Anurag Basu, H, 2004) 55

N
Nagin (The Snake, Nandlal Jaswantlal, H, 1954) 106
Namak Haram (The Disloyal, Hrishikesh Mukherjee, H, 1973) 115
Naseeb (Destiny, Manmohan Desai, H, 1981) 14
Nau Do Gyarah (Counting Numbers, Vijay Anand, H, 1958) 17
Naya Daur (New Era, B.R. Chopra, H, 1957) 106

P
Panama Pashama (Money or Love, K.S. Gopalakrishnan, Tamil, 1968) 124
Parash Pathar (The Philosopher's Stone, Satyajit Ray, Bengali, 1957) 38, 39
Pardes (In Foreign Land, Subhash Ghai, H, 1997) 69
Phagun (Month of Spring, Bibhuti Mitra, H, 1958) 106
Pitru Putra aur Dharamyudh (Father, Son and Holy War, documentary, Anand Patwardhan, H/E, 1994) 39
Prem Pujari (The Devotee of Love, Dev Anand, H, 1970) 112, 155
Purav aur Paschim (East and West, Manoj Kumar, H, 1975) 96
Pyar ke Naam Qurban (Sacrificed in the Name of Love, B. Subhash, H, 1990) 138
Pyaasa (Eternal Thirst, Guru Dutt, H, 1957) 66, 106, 107, 155

R
Raja Babu (King Babu, David Dhawan, H, 1994) 69
Raja Harishchandra (King Harishchandra, Dadasaheb Phalke, silent, 1913) 49
Ram Ke Naam (In the Name of God, documentary, Anand Patwardhan, H/E, 1992) 39
Roja (Rose, Mani Ratnam, Tamil, 1992) 97, 116
Ram Lakhan (Ram & Lakhan, Subhash Ghai, H, 1989) 82
Roti (Bread, Mehboob Khan, H, 1942) 67

S
Sahib Bibi aur Ghulam (Master, Mistress and Servant, Abrar Alvi, H, 1962) 91
Sangam (Confluence, Raj Kapoor, H, 1964) 54, 69, 77, 89, 141
Sarfarosh (They Who Sacrifice, J.M. Matthan, H, 1999) 98
Satyam Shivam Sundaram (Truth, Holiness, Beauty, Raj Kapoor, H, 1978) 19, 55, 116, 117, 155
Searchers, The (John Ford, E, 1956) 17
Shaan (The Glory, Ramesh Sippy, H, 1980) 14, 61
Shaheed Bhagat Singh (K.N. Bansal, H, 1953) 39
Shirin va Farhad (Shirin and Farhad, Abdolhossein Sepenta, silent, 1936) 137
Sholay (Flames, Ramesh Sippy, H, 1975) 48, 56, 72, 114, 115
Shree 420 (Mr.420, Raj Kapoor, H, 1955) 17, 106
Silsila (Matters of the Heart, Yash Chopra, H, 1981) 70
Sone ki Chidiya (Golden Cage, Shaheed Latif, H, 1958) 106
Son of India (Mehboob Khan, H, 1962) 101
Street Singer (Phani Majumdar, Bengali/H, 1938) 64, 103, 155
Sujata (Sujata, Bimal Roy, H, 1959) 96
Swades (The Homeland, Ashutosh Gowarikar, H, 2004) 148, 149
Swarg (Heaven, David Dhawan, H, 1990) 82

T
Taxi Driver (Chetan Anand, H, 1954) 106
Teesri Manzil (The Third Floor, Vijay Anand, H, 1966) 108, 155
Tere Ghar Ke Saamne (Opposite Your House, Vijay Anand, H, 1963) 112
Tezaab (Acid, N. Chandra, H, 1988) 82
Throw of Dice (Franz Osten, silent, 1929) 36, 37
Tridev (Three Lords, Rajiv Ray, H, 1989) 139
Trishul (Trident, Yash Chopra, H, 1978) 114
Tumsa Nahi Dekha (I Never Saw Anyone Like You, Nasir Hussain, H, 1957) 106

U
Umrao Jaan (Umrao Jaan, Muzaffar Ali, Urdu, 1981) 112, 113, 155

V
Veer-Zara (Veer & Zara, Yash Chopra, H, 2004) 35

Y
Yashoda Krishna (Yashoda and Krishna, C.S. Rao, Telugu, 1975) 81
Yuva (Youth, Mani Ratnam, H, 2004) 122

Z
Zanjeer (Chains, Prakash Mehra, H, 1973) 57, 114, 115

E = English
H = Hindi

The English translations of Hindi, Urdu, Bengali and Tamil film titles in this book are not necessarily the official translations.

SOURCES

Illustration on page 76:
Form of Beauty
The Krishna Art of B. G. Sharma
By B.V. Tripurari, Swami Tripurari
Mandala Publishing Group
Singapore/India/USA, 1998

Illustration on page 72:
The Flute and the Lotus,
Romantic Moments in Indian Poetry & Painting
By Harsha Dehejia
Grantha Corporation/Mapin Publishing
USA/India, 2002

Illustrations on pages 77, 79:
Indian Miniatures,
The Ehrenfeld Collection
By Daniel J. Ehnbom
Belser Verlag
Stuttgart/Zürich, 1988

Encyclopaedia of Indian Cinema,
New Revised Edition
By Ashish Rajadhyaksha and Paul Willemen
British Film Institute
Oxford University Press
United Kingdom, 1999

PHOTOGRAPHS

Page 44:
Kabhi Khushi Kabhie Gham, by Ayesha Monani.

Page 61:
Lata Mangeshkar and Asha Bhosle, by Gautam Rajadhyaksha.

Page 73:
Krisna in front of cinema hall, by Marijke de Vos.

Pages 122, 123:
Ayuthu Ezuthu film set, by Marijke de Vos.

Pages 122, 123:
Tamil Stars book covers by Rupa Publishers.

Page 140:
Shah Rukh Khan tour, by Jon Page/Hyphen Film Collection.

Page 141:
Shah Rukh Khan in the Netherlands, by Jörgen Caris (*Trouw*) and Guus Dubbelman (*Volkskrant*).

Page 61:
Saroj Khan, by Jitu Savlani.

Page 61:
Sonu Nigam, by Subi Samuel.

Additional images from films by the following production companies were used in this book: Yashraj, Navketan, Mehboob, Madras Talkies, RK Productions, Guru Dutt, GP Sippy, BR Chopra and others.

All other photographs by Johan Manschot.

ABOUT THE AUTHORS

Gayatri Chatterjee began her professional life as a schoolteacher. She now teaches film studies in India and abroad. Her first book, *Awaara*, received the President's Gold Medal in 1992. She wrote *Mother India* in 2002 for the British Film Institute's 'BFI Film Classics' series. Penguin India also published both these titles. Several of her articles have been published in national and international journals. Gayatri sings *Rabindrasangeet*, the music composed by the Bengali poet, painter and singer Rabindranath Tagore.

Fareeda graduated in social sciences and studied film direction at the Film and Television Institute of India, Pune. She directed her first feature film, *Kali Salwaar*, in 2001. It was shown at the international film festivals in India, Rotterdam and Gothenburg, among others. Her graduation film, *Hawa Ka Rang*, won first prize at the Turin Film Festival (1990) and was screened at various film festivals around the world. She has also worked on documentaries.

Deepa Gahlot is a freelance journalist, critic, columnist, author and editor. She has written on film, theatre, culture and women's issues. She won the National Award for Film Criticism in 1998. Her work has appeared in anthologies of cinema writing and books on cinema. She has worked on documentaries, run a features syndicate, written film scripts, been a member of film-festival juries and script committees, worked for the radio and conducted workshops.
At present, she edits the NFDC's journal *Cinema in India*, Kodak's *Images* and other publications. She has also written a book on the Bombay-based Prithvi Theatre.

Nasreen Munni Kabir is a documentary film-maker who has made several series and programmes on Hindi cinema for Channel 4 in the United Kingdom, including *Movie Mahal*, *Follow that Star* (a profile of Amitabh Bachchan), *Lata In Her Own Voice* and *How to Make a Bollywood Movie*. In 2002, she produced and directed a documentary on the making of Andrew Lloyd Webber's *Bombay Dreams* for BBC1. Nasreen is Channel 4's consultant on Indian cinema and makes the selection for its annual twenty-part Indian film season. She has also written several books, including *Guru Dutt – a Life in Cinema* (1996), *Talking Films with Javed Akhtar* (1999) and *Bollywood, the Indian Cinema Story* (2000). Nasreen has just completed two documentaries on actor Shah Rukh Khan. She was born in India and has lived most of her life in London and Paris; she organised the first major Indian film festivals in France at the Georges Pompidou Centre in 1983 and 1985. Nasreen won the first Asian Women's' Achievement Award in 1999 for her work promoting Indian cinema in the United Kingdom, and is a governor on the board of the British Film Institute.

Johan Manschot, graduate of the HKU (Art Academy, Utrecht), is an illustrator and a graphic designer. After travelling widely, he has increasingly specialised in Indian and Eastern design. He has assembled an impressive private collection of Indian film-related art that includes southern Indian film posters, records and photos. His passion for Indian film posters inspired the conception of this book. He is also establishing himself in the Netherlands as a graphic designer for Diesel jeans, Bijenkorf department store, the Tivoli venue, and the monthly MysticGrooves dance parties in Rasa and the Melkweg.

P.K. Nair, archivist, film scholar and film festival consultant, has headed the National Film Archive of India in Pune for nearly three decades. He built it up from scratch to its present international status as one of the leading film archives in Asia. He played a leading role in developing film studies in India, and is an authority on Indian cinema. He has taught extensively in India and abroad, and has guided several research scholars through their doctoral theses on various aspects of the art form. He has served as jury member of several national and international film festivals, and continues to be actively involved in film archiving, and the training of young archivists, film-makers and film critics. A dedicated film historian and film scholar, he has made an in-depth study of Indian silent cinema and written extensively on various aspects of the evolution of cinema in India.

Sudha Rajagopalan, originally from Bombay, is a doctor in Russian/Soviet history at Indiana University (Bloomington) in the USA. Inspired by her own attachment to Indian films and the spontaneity and passion with which people in the former Soviet Union always engaged her on the subject, Rajagopalan was eager to document and analyse the pivotal role of these films in Soviet history. Her work investigates the function of Indian popular cinema in post-Stalinist Soviet society and is based on extensive ethnographic and archival research in Russia. She currently lives in Leiden, the Netherlands.

Brahmanand Singh is a Bombay-based writer and film-maker. He has published stories, poems and essays in India and abroad, written screenplays, and made documentaries and short films. His films are typified by their lyrical qualities.
Prominent among his documentaries are *Ashgari Bai* (Echoes of Silence, 1997), about a legendary octogenarian *dhrupad* singer,[1] and *A Burden of Love* (2004), about Alzheimer's disease. In addition, he has made many commissioned corporate documentaries. His films have been screened at various international film festivals and on Doordarshan, the Indian national television network. He has directed and written for a number of television series.
He studies Hindustani classical music with Ustad Aslam Hussain Khan, a prominent contemporary musician, and has written a great deal on various music genres – from classical to popular cinema music.

Soudhamini is a film-maker, film scholar and critic from Chennai. She has made several documentaries, which include *Saga of a Poet* (2002) on the life and works of the poet Subramania Bharathi; a short film on education for Tribals,[2] *Going to School* (2001); a mini-series for television on artists and patronage, *The Invisible Flame* (1997); and a feature-length documentary called *Pitru Chayya*: Shadows of our Forefather (1991), inspired by the classical musician M.D. Ramanathan. Soudhamini teaches at some of the premier film-study programmes in India, including that of her alma mater, the Film and Television Institute of India, Pune.

Hadi Tehrani, is a theatre-maker, film actor, critic and scriptwriter from Iran. He founded an experimental theatre school in the Iranian province Khorasan. Tehrani has lived for the last ten years in the Netherlands, as an asylum seeker.

Marijke de Vos, graduate of the Rietveld Academie (Art Academy, Amsterdam), is a film programmer and theatre researcher. Since 1990 she programmed numerous Indian films – from the early years to the latest blockbusters and art films – for the annual Cinema India festival in the Royal Tropical Institute, Amsterdam. She is an adviser on Indian cinema to organisations such as the Dutch broadcasting company NPS, public television and several cultural festivals. She has written on Indian cinema and given master classes, and lectures on Indian cinema at the universities of Leiden, Rotterdam and Amsterdam. She is a member of the selection committee of the Jan Vrijman Fund for IDFA (International Documentary Festival Amsterdam).

[1] *Dhrupad* is a form of Indian classical music.
[2] India's tribal peoples.

COLOPHON

KIT Publishers
Mauritskade 63
P.O. Box 95001
1090 HA Amsterdam
The Netherlands
publishers@kit.nl
www.kit.nl/publishers

Concept and Realisation:
Johan Manschot and Marijke de Vos

Author and Editor: Marijke de Vos
Art Direction and Layout: Johan Manschot

Text Editor: Steve Green
Production: Meester & De Jonge, Lochem

Cover: Rekha, detail from **Ghungroo ki Awaaz** (1981)

© 2005 KIT Publishers, Amsterdam
All rights reserved. No part of this book may be reproduced, stored in a retrieval system, or transmitted in any form, or by any means, electronic or otherwise, without prior written permission of the publisher.

Every effort has been made to contact all copyright holders: the publisher will be glad to make good in future editions any errors or omissions brought to their attention.

ISBN 90 6832 186 2
NUR 652

PREVIOUS PAGES:
Do Raaste
Deewaar and **Babul**
Lagaan and **Sarfarosh**